Making ALL Kids *Smarter*

Strategies That Help All Students Reach Their Highest Potential

JOHN DELANDTSHEER

CORWIN
A SAGE Company

For information:

Corwin
A SAGE Company
2455 Teller Road
Thousand Oaks, California 91320
(800) 233–9936
Fax: (800) 417–2466
www.corwin.com

SAGE Ltd.
1 Oliver's Yard
55 City Road
London EC1Y 1SP
United Kingdom

SAGE India Pvt. Ltd.
B 1/I 1 Mohan Cooperative
Industrial Area
Mathura Road,
New Delhi 110 044
India

SAGE Asia-Pacific Pte. Ltd.
33 Pekin Street #02–01
Far East Square
Singapore 048763

Printed in the United States of America

Library of Congress Cataloging-in-Publication Data

DeLandtsheer, John.
Making all kids smarter : strategies that help all students reach their highest potential/ John DeLandtsheer.
    p. cm.
Includes bibliographical references and index.
ISBN 978-1-4129-8903-9 (pbk.)
    1. Academic achievement. 2. Motivation in education. 3. Teacher-student relationships. I. Title.

LB1062.6.D45 2011
371.39—dc22   2010034891

This book is printed on acid-free paper.

10 11 12 13 14 10 9 8 7 6 5 4 3 2 1

Acquisitions Editor:	Jessica Allan
Associate Editor:	Allison Scott
Editorial Assistant:	Lisa Whitney
Production Editor:	Amy Schroller
Permissions Editor:	Karen Ehrmann
Copy Editor:	Tina Hardy
Typesetter:	C&M Digitals (P) Ltd.
Proofreader:	Eleni-Maria Georgiou
Indexer:	Judy Hunt
Cover Designer:	Karine Hovsepian

Contents

Preface

When I was approached to write this book, the focus was to be on gifted students and how to *make smart kids smarter*. As the book evolved, however, it became clear to me and to my editor at Corwin that there was a definite need for a book about making ALL kids smarter. While the focus still is on gifted and high-ability students, this book is about activities and instructional strategies designed to be compatible with how the brain processes information. Therefore, the content is about more than just making our bright kids brighter; it's about making more and more kids smarter.

With the passage of the No Child Left Behind Act (NCLB), the mandate for schools has been to increase the performance of the lowest achieving students so that all children reach a minimal proficiency level. More than a decade later, NCLB continues to influence educational practices as standardized assessments are used to determine proficiency levels. However, in my current work with teachers, students, administrators, and parents, it appears that test scores have become the goal of teaching rather than an indicator of performance. This isn't a book about raising test scores. Rather, it is a guide with strategies and activities for *teaching kids to be thinkers*, helping them become smarter in a variety of ways. Happily, a positive consequence of utilizing these strategies is that test scores do improve. That has been the experience at my school and at other schools where these strategies have been implemented.

Much of the terminology in this book is from the world of gifted and talented education. This is because the philosophy of working with our brightest students has always been to challenge them in meaningful ways. Applying these terms to a broader group can only increase the opportunities students will have to think more deeply and meaningfully about content. After 40 years as an educator, I have come to believe that we don't expect nearly as much from some students as we do others. I'm convinced that holding such diminished expectations for some students is a form of discrimination that we should examine carefully.

This book is about taking the strategies previously reserved for our gifted and brightest children and presenting them to all of our students, regardless of ability levels. This philosophy guided me as a teacher, principal, administrator, and university instructor and it continues to do so now in my role as a consultant working with educators in districts across the country.

I hope you will find this book both informative and liberating. I trust it will bring back the enthusiasm and joy that you experienced when you entered this profession and that, consequently, your job will become more interesting, meaningful and, dare I say, FUN!

Enjoy!!!

Acknowledgments

This book could not have been written without the tremendous help from my wife, Joelle, who worked and reworked every sentence to make sure my words came across clearly and concisely. Her experience as a teacher and administrator contributed much to the clarity of this book.

The wonderful staff, students, and parents of Mariposa and Kimberly Elementary Schools in Redlands, California, have earned my gratitude and respect for being so accepting of my ideas and approaches over the years. The teachers tried so many of the strategies contained in this book and gave me honest feedback as to what worked and what needed to be modified, and they even shared ways they adapted and improved upon them. Working with a staff of such exemplary educators has been the highlight of my educational career and I thank each of them.

My colleague and friend, Margee Fuller, a teacher and GATE coordinator at Mariposa Elementary School and fellow gifted and talented education (GATE) instructor at University of California Riverside, deserves special thanks for sharing so many of her teaching strategies, more than a few of which have found their way into this book. Bob Hodges, my superintendent for many years in Redlands Unified School District (USD), has my utmost respect and is to be commended for his educational leadership. He allowed me the freedom and support to grow professionally as a principal, as well as opportunities to pursue my passion and commitment to gifted education and brain-compatible learning.

I also wish to acknowledge all the teachers, administrators, and parents who have participated in my workshops through the years, sharing their feedback, case studies, and ideas. I never fail to learn something new from each them and I appreciate their ongoing support. I would be remiss if I neglected to thank a special group of friends and colleagues who live in my hometown of Big Bear Lake, California. Their children were some of my first students and I've taken pleasure in watching them grow into responsible adults and I still enjoy hearing from them.

Finally, I would like to thank our son, Dr. John Kimball DeLandtsheer, who taught my wife and me so much about what goes on inside the head of a gifted youngster. Raising him has been quite an experience for the three of us! Listening to what he had to say about school, both how he was motivated and what turned him off, helped me understand what we teachers need to do in order to make education meaningful, interesting, and engaging for our students.

About the Author

 **John DeLandtsheer** has been an educator for over 40 years. He has taught elementary, middle, and high school in public schools and at the university level in California. For the past 20 years, his focus has been in gifted education and conducting teacher certification in this area. John received his BA in English from Whittier College and his MA in School Leadership and Administration from California State University at San Bernardino. As an administrator, he has coordinated gifted programs at both the district and county levels. John served as a principal for 16 years at two elementary schools in Redlands Unified School District, both of which were honored as California Distinguished Schools. Kimberly Elementary was a bilingual magnet school and Mariposa Elementary was a demonstration site for gifted and talented students during that time. John taught in the GATE Certificate Program through the University of California, at the Riverside campus, for over 20 years. Currently, he travels as a consultant for his company JD Seminars, Inc. to provide staff development seminars in higher level thinking skills for all students and teacher certification for gifted and talented education. Over the past 20 years, he has provided training to nearly 2,000 teachers and administrators. John and his wife, Joelle, live in the small rural community of Fawnskin, in the Southern California Mountains, overlooking beautiful Big Bear Lake. Their son and his wife and two grandchildren reside in Redding, California.

This book is dedicated to Joelle, John K., Kim, Mason, and Brooke.

1 The Gifted Child

INTRODUCTION

Go get a piece of paper. Now, write down the name of someone whose gifts, talents, abilities, intellect, and contributions you admire. It can be a famous person, a dead person, a person who made a difference in your personal life. Now, here is the question for you: *How well did that person do in school?* Did she get 100% on spelling tests each week? Did he graduate at the top of the class? Did she get an A on that science fair project? Did he go to an Ivy League university? Perhaps you aren't sure. The person I most admire didn't even finish high school. He was viewed by his teachers as lacking in imagination. He came from a family where his father was very strict and oppressive. As an adult, he had a drinking problem and was a chain smoker. Many of the people who worked for him felt he was a very difficult boss who was brutal in his criticism of their work. On the upside, he was a great father and husband. He was generous, often taking no salary so that his employees could be paid. Have you guessed the person I most admire? It's Walt Disney. The point of this exercise is to remind us at the outset that *giftedness is not always about school performance.* School is such a small part of the lives of our gifted students; their minds often are elsewhere. Some gifted students might not be *good students* but they could be *excellent scholars.* Just keep this in mind as we examine, *Who are the gifted?*

IDENTIFYING GIFTEDNESS

Many experts have a difficult time agreeing on a definition of giftedness. However, most would identify gifted kids as the *smart kids.* How smart are they? Well, giftedness generally means those students who score at the top 3–5% on a test of intellectual ability. However, the last two decades have seen a shift in our understanding of how to identify gifted students. Many states offer special funds to provide programs for those students with very high abilities. In some states, these students are referred to as GATE (gifted and talented education), or TAG (talented and gifted), or by some other acronym. For the purposes of this book, I refer to these students as *gifted* or *GATE*. Three criteria often are used to qualify a student for a gifted program:

1. High performance on an intelligence test

2. High performance on a test of academic skills

3. Close alignment to a series of characteristic behaviors of the gifted

Put together, these three criteria represent a profile of a gifted student. This triangulation of identification components was given the name *The Three P's of GATE Identification* by a colleague and friend of mine, Kim LaPorte Johnson. The following chart shows how this looks:

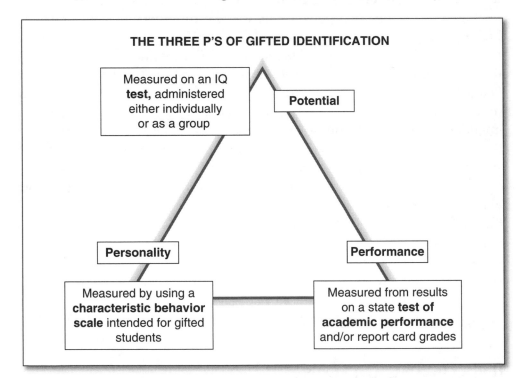

THE THREE P'S OF GIFTED IDENTIFICATION

Measured on an IQ **test,** administered either individually or as a group

Potential

Personality

Performance

Measured by using a **characteristic behavior scale** intended for gifted students

Measured from results on a state **test of academic performance** and/or report card grades

Because students are identified for gifted programs according to criteria set by each state educational agency, or even by separate school districts within a state, a student identified as gifted in New York might not qualify in Nevada or Connecticut, or vice versa. In addition, a student qualifying in Anaheim, California, might not qualify in Santa Ana, a city right next door. Although differing identification criteria may be quite confusing for parents who look upon giftedness as a *permanent label*, the logic of this identification process is quite valid once it is examined. According to practice, children are identified as gifted within the community in which they live because each region seeks to find the top 3–5% of its children for a gifted program.

IDENTIFYING FIVE AREAS OF GIFTEDNESS

There are five major areas in which a student might be identified as gifted. Most states require that *general intellectual ability* is one of the areas served. Most educational agencies also serve students in a *specific academic ability* category as well (usually language arts or math), because identification is based upon the state standardized achievement test. The other three areas (*creative thinking, leadership,* and *visual and performing arts*), are more difficult to define and, therefore, it's not as easy to identify and serve students appropriately in these areas.

FIVE AREAS OF GIFTED IDENTIFICATION

1. **General Intellectual Ability**
   - This is determined by an IQ test (the major criterion in many states).
   - The following areas of intellectual ability usually are assessed:
     o Verbal
     o Mathematical/Quantitative
     o Spatial
   - Students are not expected to perform equally well in all three areas.

2. **Creative Thinking**
   - This is determined by observation and a characteristic behavior scale.
   - Some of the following characteristics usually are addressed:
     o An affinity for creative problem solving
     o A desire to be different
     o A strong and sophisticated sense of humor

3. **Leadership**
   - This is determined by observation and a characteristic behavior scale.
   - Some of the following characteristics often are assessed:
     o Popular; well-liked by peers
     o Self-confident
     o Organized
     o Fluent and concise self-expression

(Continued)

(Continued)

4. Specific Academic Ability
- Determined by test scores on district and state achievement tests
- Considered an excellent student in at least one academic area
- Considered a high performing student in school

5. Visual and Performing Arts
- Often determined by portfolio or audition
- Significantly accomplished in one or more of the designated areas: art, drama, music, and/or dance

Adapted from the California State Department of Education

IDENTIFYING AREAS YOU CAN SERVE

Because GATE identification is a multifaceted process, students should be assessed in several areas. However, a major caution relates to how a student qualifies for a gifted program. I would advise an educational agency to refrain from identifying students in an area in which it is not prepared to provide an adequate program. Far too often, students qualifying for GATE in the visual and performing arts are placed in an advanced math class with students of strong academic ability, only to struggle and often fail. How successful are students likely to be if they possess advanced science abilities and are placed in a class designed for those with exceptional music talent? *Bottom line: For any of the areas in which a school district identifies gifted students, it should be prepared to provide an appropriate program for those students.* This service should *be over and above* what is provided for other students. At the very least, an educational agency should provide a strong program for those students who qualify for the gifted program because of their intellectual or academic abilities. As a next step, I encourage school districts to develop programs which address the other categories of giftedness.

Looking at visual and performing arts, for example, a student who is identified as *gifted* should expect more than regular classroom art or school chorus. Lessons with noted artists, inclusion in a community orchestra, or performing with a local theater group are examples of possible *above and beyond* opportunities in the visual and performing arts.

What does a school district offer specifically for students who are gifted in leadership ability—student council? Working with local community leaders, being mentored by a government official, and attending leadership conferences could qualify as *over and above* services. *Bottom line: If you can't provide services in an area, then don't identify for it!* Instead, why not develop a program?

POTENTIAL VERSUS PERFORMANCE

Another issue related to gifted identification often is expressed by teachers who might have a student in class who *couldn't rub two dendrites together if life depended upon it,* but who qualified for GATE some years past. What we do know about giftedness is quite interesting—both *potential and performance* are dynamic, changing over time. A student might qualify for GATE in second grade but, if tested again in a year or so, he might not qualify. This changing situation can become a nightmare for administering gifted programs, so most educational agencies follow the practice of *once gifted, always gifted,* even though that is not always true. However, the opposite situation can occur. A student assessed for placement in a gifted program in third grade might not qualify then, but when tested again in fourth grade, she qualifies. Why is this? Many factors come into play when a student is assessed: dynamics of the testing situation, a student's health or confidence on that day, maturity, and so forth. Who knows? So, most educational agencies operate on the premise that once students are identified, they remain in the gifted program. Such a position makes things easier both from an administrative standpoint and also for public relations.

GATE students who underperform may not lose their *gifted status* but they very well could lose their *giftedness.*

DEFINING GIFTEDNESS

Before going any further in this book, let's take a moment to define what is meant by *giftedness.* We know it can be measured on an intelligence test by scoring at the top 3–5%. However, what does *giftedness* mean beyond a test score? Since this is my book I get to choose the definition that has worked for me over the past 40 years and the one I use with the teachers in my seminars. It's from Abe Tannenbaum, a respected researcher and advocate for gifted education since the 1960s:

> Giftedness in children denotes their potential for becoming critically acclaimed performers or exemplary producers of ideas in spheres of activity that enhance the moral, physical, emotional, social, intellectual or aesthetic life of humanity.

STRESSING CONTRIBUTION

If you accept Tannenbaum's definition, then being gifted isn't about *receiving* a gift; it's more about *giving* a gift. As I explain to participants in my seminars, I believe there is an obligation attached to being gifted. This obligation is associated with the concept of *contribution*. People of high abilities have a responsibility to make this world a better place. This obligation translates itself into a variety of behaviors: tolerance, empathy, intellectualism, patience, and honesty, along with problem-solving ability and ethical behavior.

When parents say, "My child is gifted, what does she get?" I try to turn this attitude around by saying, "Your child will receive a high quality education from a GATE certified teacher who will bring out her gifts and talents. Our expectation is that your child will, in the future, contribute her gifts and talents to benefit others." I always have emphasized the concept of *paying it forward*. An exercise I used the first week of school when I taught special classes for intellectually gifted students is described here:

> You have all been identified as gifted, which means you are among the top 3–5% of all students in mental ability. What are you going to do with this gift to make our classroom and this school a better place? Please sit down with a partner and list five things you can do to share your gift for the betterment of our school and community. These will become our goals for the year.

As a teacher, and later as a principal, my goal for students was to see their names listed on that scrap of paper when someone in the future asked, "Who do you admire?" As an educator, what I wish for all students is for them to be on *The List* of people whose gifts, talents, contributions, and abilities are so outstanding that they are remembered as being *exceptional*. Being rich and famous, to me, is not nearly as important as making a positive difference in the lives of others. Hopefully, you will agree with me and instill in your students this strong sense of *contribution and commitment*. It sort of makes getting an A+ on the weekly spelling test a bit mundane, doesn't it?

THE CAUSES OF GIFTEDNESS

As we further examine *who are the gifted,* the question comes up, "What actually causes giftedness?" Is it genetic, or is it environmental, or is it simply an aberration? Although much has been written about the research in this area, little has been discussed for fear of offending someone. There are two schools of thought: one is *genetic* and the other is *environmental.* Here is the simple *genetic* explanation: Smart people marry smart people and have smart children. Generally, this is true. Occasionally, however, two very smart people will have a very dull child. Likewise, two people of very average or low intelligence may have a brilliant child. In biology, this phenomenon is called a *mutation.*

Another cause of giftedness is *environmental,* the belief that you can *make* a child gifted by exposing him or her to a variety of enriching experiences, beginning at an early age. Studies have confirmed that this does work for younger children; however, their intelligence seems to *level off* when they reach about fourth grade, or age 9 to 10. This does not mean that parents shouldn't play Mozart to their unborn child. It can't hurt, but it probably won't help too much in the long run. We do know that children whose parents engaged them in conversation at an early age and encouraged them to "use your words" generally are smarter than those who have not had these experiences. Paul Slocumb and Ruby Payne (2000) have discussed this topic at great length in their book, *Removing the Mask: Giftedness in Poverty.* This book is worth a first and a second read! However, we all know there are exceptions to almost everything and my cousin George is an example. Although exposed to an enriched language experience at an early age, he didn't speak until he was almost seven. Now, he is a nuclear physicist. Go figure.

APPRECIATING UNIQUENESS

Whatever the cause of giftedness, some kids simply are smarter than others. However, teachers need to worry less about this issue and more about making all kids smarter. While all children have their own gifts and talents, this is not to be confused with the *clinical definition* of gifted and talented which applies to the top 3–5% of students. If we define giftedness as *very high ability and potential,* some students, unfortunately, are not gifted. Once we accept this fact, we then can proceed to meet the needs of our gifted children who have special needs of their own.

Some teachers and administrators tend to speak in platitudes hoping to make everyone feel good: "All students are gifted." There is a sense that it isn't *fair* that some students have it all: they are highly intelligent, excellent athletes, good looking, and simply nice kids. *Don't you just hate 'em?* Of course we don't! However, we are fixated on the concept of *fairness.* We want life to be fair and it simply isn't.

ELIMINATING THE "F" WORD

As a teacher and administrator, I have heard students use the "F" word in school, which isn't allowed. I would like to suggest banning another "F" word: *fair.* If we are concerned that it isn't *fair* that some kids are smarter than others, then we fall victim to the ever-present *Pity Principle* which has governed our profession for over three decades. The *Pity Principle* implies  that we can't intervene or provide extra service to members of any group unless we *pity* them in some way: they are poor, they don't speak English, they are disabled, they are a minority, or they are cognitively delayed. While there are programs for these groups of children, we fall short when it comes to investing in programs for those who are capable. *Are gifted children expected to fend for themselves?* Sometimes, it appears so. When I worked for the County Office of Education, I had the opportunity to conduct nearly a hundred *time-on-task analyses* in as many classrooms as part of *Effective Schools Research.* What always concerned me was that the most common off-task behavior of gifted and high-ability students was waiting. The vast majority of gifted students I observed in regular classrooms spent nearly 20% of their day waiting. Simple arithmetic helped me calculate this alarming statistic: By the time a gifted child graduates from high school, he has spent two years of his educational career waiting for others to finish. Waiting for the rest to *get it* is the single most nonproductive behavior experienced by our gifted students. As you read further, however, strategies will be provided to help remedy this situation.

THE GATE CLASSROOM AS THE BEST CLASSROOM

Since we are on the topic of placement for gifted students, we need to discuss another *elephant in the living room.* As a retired principal, I fully understand the problems associated with clustering gifted students together in the same classroom. Soon, the perception is that the GATE class is the *best class.* Parents of non-GATE students may begin to resent such a special class or try to get their own children into the class. How interesting it is that these parents don't resent the special education classes. In any event, principals have a difficult time when it comes to the placement of gifted youngsters because they want to please everyone. As a result, principals fall victim to the *Tootsie Roll Approach,* distributing gifted students equally in each class, much like Halloween candy, *one for you, one for you, and one for you.*

GROUPING PRACTICES FOR THE GIFTED

Let's examine what the research says about grouping gifted students together. Sally Reis, a renowned researcher in gifted education at the University of Connecticut, has conducted studies about placement of students. She has described various instructional practices and their impact on GATE students. I've combined Reis's findings and added my own descriptions of what I've observed in schools related to GATE grouping practices. This information is outlined in the chart that follows:

GROUPING PRACTICES FOR GIFTED STUDENTS

- **Full-day placement** in a class comprised entirely of gifted students, taught by a teacher trained to provide instruction for gifted students
- GATE **cluster classes** where about 10 students, irrespective of total class size, are identified GATE and the remainder of the class is a heterogeneous group
- A **pull-out program** where gifted students leave the classroom daily for an hour, or perhaps for a half-day once a week, to do advanced studies with a teacher trained to work with gifted students
- **Distribution of gifted students** among all the teachers at a grade level (the Tootsie Roll approach), also called the *Do Nothing Option!*
- **Part-time grouping** of students during the day where gifted and talented students have a special class matched to their area of expertise (advanced math, English, or science; music or art)
- **After school and Saturday specialized activities** designed for gifted students (not particularly effective since it assumes gifted students need to be challenged only *after* school hours)

Reis's research indicated that a pull-out program with a highly trained teacher might work best for GATE students. However, my personal experience with the current standards-based curriculum is that gifted students in a pull-out program feel somewhat disassociated from classmates. Also, it is a common expectation that GATE students either make up the work they missed while out of the regular classroom (*Isn't that fun!!!!*) or, if they are excused from the work, they are expected to have mastered anything taught while they were away.

Another major drawback of pull-out programs is the cost. Not too many educational agencies can afford additional staff to provide GATE pull-out classes. In short, while GATE pull-out programs have been successful in the past, they may not work as well with current budget constraints. Of all the options Reis outlines, clustering seems to be the most common approach to grouping gifted students that is being used currently.

Here are some thoughts about *clustering gifted students* that should be considered:

CLUSTERING GATE STUDENTS

- All cluster classes need to be taught by a GATE trained/certified teacher.
- A cluster is about 10 students. Here are some guidelines for placement:
  - At fourth grade, if there are only five GATE students in the school, then all of them should go into one classroom.
  - If there are 14 gifted students in fifth grade, then I would put them all in the same class.
  - With 20 gifted students at a grade level, you could form two GATE clusters, rather than putting all 20 students in one class.
- The remainder of the GATE cluster class can be composed of a *heterogeneous* group of students. While some schools fill out the GATE cluster classes with high performing students, as a former principal, I did not want to deplete the other classes of all the high performing students.
- Students with mild to moderate learning disabilities may be included within the heterogeneous group of students in the GATE cluster classes. Reis cautions, however, that special education students with the greatest academic difficulties might not be placed in the GATE cluster class. Just a reminder, 8–10% of our gifted students also have learning disabilities. They are often referred to as *double-labeled* or *twice-exceptional.*

It is essential that GATE cluster classes have a sufficient number of gifted students placed together to create what is considered a *critical mass* so that they can interact with each other. Also, while four or five gifted students can be overlooked easily in a classroom, it is more difficult to ignore a cluster of 10.

WHAT WE KNOW ABOUT INTELLIGENCE

Since the goal of education is to make all kids smarter, then an examination of what we know currently about intelligence might give us some insight into how we can help students reach their highest potential. Since we know we CAN make kids smarter, and that intelligence is not static but ever-changing, the more we know about how smart kids differ from others, the more we are able to make more kids smarter!

Stephen Ceci, psychologist and professor of developmental psychology at Cornell University, is considered an expert in the development of intelligence and memory. His article, entitled *IQ Intelligence: The Surprising Truth* (2001), presents 12 supported facts about intelligence compiled from earlier works. Some of the highlights of his findings are displayed in the box that follows:

FACTS ABOUT INTELLIGENCE

1. **IQ correlates with some simple abilities**—The higher your intelligence, the faster you process information and the quicker you can solve problems.

2. **IQ is affected by school attendance**—The longer you remain in school, the smarter you become. Staying in school can prevent your IQ from slipping. IQ declines over summer vacation and with lack of performance. For each year of high school not completed, there is an average loss of 1.8 IQ points. Delaying schooling has adverse effects on IQ.

3. **IQ is not influenced by birth order**—There is no correlation between birth order and intelligence. However, as a group, smarter people tend to have fewer children than those of lower intelligence.

4. **IQ is related to breast-feeding**—By age 3, breast-fed babies have an IQ that is from three to eight points higher than bottle-fed babies. (This may be related to the amount of time a mother and child spend together while nursing. It also may be that the immune factors in mothers' milk prevent children from getting diseases that deplete energy and impair early learning.)

5. **IQ varies by birth date**—Students born late in the year, as a group, show lower IQ scores. For each year of schooling completed, there is an IQ gain of approximately 3.5 points.

6. **IQ evens out with age**—Siblings who are raised separately may have marked differences in IQ when they are younger. However, once they reach adulthood, their IQs are more similar. (This probably is due to genetic factors which take priority over environmental ones.)

7. **Intelligence is plural, not singular**—Three kinds of intelligence are generally recognized: spatial, verbal, and analytical/mathematical. A fourth type, practical/common sense, also has been noted by the author. Other recognized GATE authorities have embraced the theory of *multiple intelligences*.

8. **IQ is correlated to head size**—Based upon IQ tests, the larger a person's head, the smarter he is. Cranial volume seems to be correlated to IQ. (This correlation was discovered in the Armed Forces where every inductee is given an IQ test and also measured for a helmet.)

(Continued)

(Continued)

9. **Intelligence scores are predictive of real-world outcomes**—Over their lifetimes, people who have completed more school tend to earn more. College graduates earn over $800,000 more than high school graduates. Those with professional degrees earn nearly $1,600,000 more than college graduates. As a rule, the higher a person's intellectual ability, the higher her earnings.

10. **Intelligence is context-dependent**—A person can be really smart in one area and very average in other areas. Being able to reason complexly depends upon what each person is required to think about.

11. **IQ is on the rise**—Average IQ has risen 20 points with every generation. We are smarter than our parents, and our children very likely will be smarter than we are. The bar continues to rise.

12. **IQ may be influenced by the school cafeteria menu**—Diet influences brain functioning. *Eat your fish. It's brain food!* A 14% increase in IQ was noted after preservatives were removed from the cafeteria menu in New York City public schools. This improvement was greatest among remedial students.

SOME FINAL THOUGHTS

We need to recognize that some students are more intelligent than others. However, instructional strategies previously reserved for the brightest students can be used effectively with a wider range of student abilities. Many times, the entire class can participate successfully in an activity that is appropriate for students of high ability. All students can benefit from being asked to think critically, to examine content in depth, to connect content being learned to other content, and to move faster through the content.

As you read the information in succeeding chapters and use the strategies presented, don't think just about your *gifted youngsters,* think about *all your students.* Some youngsters will grasp the concepts very readily; others may labor a bit, while some students might struggle a lot. However, the more frequently you provide students with opportunities to stretch their thinking, the more adept they will become at it. Conversely, if students are never asked to extend their thinking, we teachers are doing them a disservice. Every student has a right to be exposed to the most rigorous content.

The next chapter is about how the brain works, with specific strategies to use in a brain-compatible classroom. By regularly using the strategies in the following chapters, teachers will increase opportunities for deeper thinking and more meaningful learning for all students.

2 Brain-Compatible Classrooms

INTRODUCTION

Discussing brain-based learning will help the reader understand how the strategies included in this book are based on the way the brain works. Therefore, these strategies may be used effectively with a wide range of students. For several years during my teaching career, I worked with gifted students in the morning and with Title I remedial students in the afternoon. Many times, I used the *same* activities for both groups. The major difference I found in how the two groups processed information was the element of *think time*. While gifted students made connections far more rapidly and deeply, given additional time and encouragement, the remedial students were successful as well. In my seminars, I frequently remind teachers that *just because a child cannot read does not mean the child cannot think!*

THE HUMAN BRAIN AND LEARNING

Numerous books have been written on brain research over the past two decades. It is a current topic in education and one that has intrigued me for years. Publications related to brain research from the authors noted here were used as background for this chapter.

PUBLICATIONS RELATED TO BRAIN RESEARCH

I'm especially indebted to the following authors for their publications on brain research, which have influenced my own work with teachers and students.

- Barbara Clark, author of *Growing Up Gifted* (1997), for her articles and lectures on current cognitive research
- Leslie Hart, for his book, *Human Brain, Human Learning* (1983), and related articles about how the brain works related to learning
- Pat Wolfe, author of *Brain Matters: Translating Research into Classroom Practice* (2001), for her presentations and writings on brain physiology
- Eric Jensen, for his books, *Teaching With the Brain in Mind* (1998), *Super Teaching* (2008), and other publications related to brain-based learning
- Renate and Geoffrey Caine for their book, *Making Connections: Teaching and the Human Brain* (1990), which is about brain science related to learning
- Merrill Harmin, author of *Inspiring Active Learning: A Complete Handbook for Today's Teachers* (2006), whose writings have shown me how to enrich teaching for all students

BRAIN PHYSIOLOGY

So, what do teachers need to know about the brain? Well, let's start with the *physical brain*. We know the brain is divided into *two hemispheres*. The left hemisphere controls the right side of the body and the right hemisphere controls the left side. Because it is so compensatory, the brain is very adaptable. It's always learning, provided it is given what it needs to learn: *nutrition and stimulation*. We know that most of the brain's growth occurs between birth and age four. This is the time when the brain is most *hungry* for learning and when brain cells, or neurons, grow dendrite branches and make their connections most rapidly. *Growing dendrites actually is what makes a person smarter.*

THE BRAIN

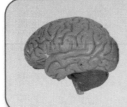

While the brain weighs only three pounds, it uses 20% of the body's blood supply. Maybe that's why a tiny cut on a child's head bleeds like it is a gash a foot long! The brain also is a glutton for oxygen, using 25% of the body's supply, so take a few deep breaths and give your brain a shot of O_2.

The more branches on the *neuron tree*, the smarter the student. I used to tell my students, "Do it for your dendrites!" whenever they were confronted with difficult work. We know that the brain is a pattern-seeking device that is designed to find relationships between sensory inputs. Learning actually is the growth of these dendrites as they seek out other neurons to make connections. Remembering back to your high school physiology classes, you will recall that neurological impulses travel across a synaptic gap between the dendrite and the axon of another brain cell. This electrochemical spray is what transmits the impulse to make learning happen.

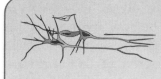

BRAIN CELLS OR NEURONS

The neuron is much like a tree with branches, a trunk, and roots. The more *branches* on the neuron tree, the more connections the cell can make with other cells. Therefore, telling students, "Do it for your dendrites!" helps remind them how *rigorous* and *meaningful* schoolwork is designed to make them *smarter*, not just to keep them busy or to raise test scores.

BUILDING DENDRITE CONNECTIONS

Dendrite connections can be made throughout a person's life, however, the time of most brain growth is during early childhood. We also know that brain cells grow during the *output* phase of learning, when kids are doing something. That is, for children to get smarter, they have to be actively involved. So, what are some of the output activities for students that will grow dendrites? The chart that follows illustrates the three output activities related to learning content:

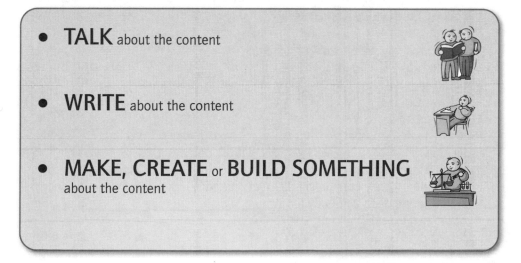

- **TALK** about the content

- **WRITE** about the content

- **MAKE, CREATE** or **BUILD SOMETHING** about the content

ACTIVE LEARNING

Unless students are engaged in one of the three output activities shown in the box, they aren't growing dendrites. Simply thinking about the content may not be sufficient for most students to get smarter. At any rate, *thinking* about it certainly doesn't tell the teacher anything about how much the student knows about the content. A critical understanding related to learning is that *whoever does the work gets smarter.* Therefore, if teachers are doing all the managing of the classroom, the organization and the planning, then *they* are the ones who are getting smarter, not the students. Whenever teachers or parents do something for youngsters that the kids are capable of doing for themselves, I believe the children are robbed of the opportunity to get smarter. We teachers may want to ask ourselves, "How many of the tasks we perform during the school day could be done by the students instead of by us?" Remember: *Whoever does the work gets smarter!* Teachers are already smart. They have the diploma and the credentials to prove it. Now, it's time to let the kids get smart.

ADDITIONAL FACTS ABOUT THE BRAIN

- The brain weighs about three pounds. It's the texture of a ripe avocado and the size of a cantaloupe, mainly made up of fat. In fact, the fat is very close to fish oil in its chemical makeup.
- Because the brain periodically *self prunes,* if the neurons are not used for their assigned tasks, the brain cells are reallocated or absorbed back into the system. *Use it or lose it!*
- The most important cells in the body are the brain cells or neurons. These cells never divide after birth but can grow through *budding,* like a hydra. Most adult neurons stay in the same area of the brain; they just extend or branch out. The neurons of children, however, do *move about* depending on where they are needed. As you age, you lose over 10,000 brain cells a day. However, you have billions, so it's not that critical. In the studies of the aged, mental stimulation with content, as well as interactions with people, can slow the loss of brain cells.
- The density of the brain is not as critical as the number and complexity of the branching. Brain weight doesn't seem to matter either.
- Different areas of the brain develop and mature at different rates. The brain develops from the brain stem up. This means that we develop our *fright-flight* response first and our *problem-solving, logical thinking* skills later.
- By ages 10 to 13, the brain still is in its developmental stages. Specifically, the fibers in the *corpus callosum,* the bundle of nerves connecting the two hemispheres, have not fully matured for optimum learning. For example, many eighth graders are not ready for algebra, a discipline that requires integration of the two brain hemispheres. In contrast, the brain of a seven-year-old is ideal for learning a foreign language. Unfortunately, by the time foreign language is taught in middle school, the brain cells devoted to language acquisition have long since been reassigned to other tasks. No wonder learning a foreign language is difficult for many older students.

LEFT AND RIGHT BRAIN DOMINANCE

Recent brain studies have pointed to the fact that the brain is very compensatory. That is, it has the capability of making modifications, depending upon circumstances. Early studies focused on the importance of left and right *hemisphere dominance*, while more recent research indicates that there is far more *crossover* between the hemispheres than was previously believed. Therefore, we need to avoid labeling the left hemisphere as exclusively *logical* and the right hemisphere as exclusively *creative*. In general, both sides of the brain are used, to some degree, in nearly every human activity. However, there still are some basic differences between the left and the right hemispheres.

USING THE LEFT AND RIGHT SIDES OF THE BRAIN

 The left brain is mostly logical, sequential, and analytical. Generally, it is used to process parts in sequence, such as reading a novel or following the steps for solving a long division problem. Musicians process music in the left hemisphere. The left brain deals with details. Girls have earlier left brain hemisphere maturation than boys, which is why they tend to read earlier and are more verbal than boys at the same age.

 The right brain is more random, conceptual, and abstract. Generally, it is used for creative activities such as drawing a picture or spatial tasks like putting together a puzzle. It is the more undisciplined side of the brain, subject to anger and worry. Sensory input is processed in the right hemisphere. Boys tend to use the right side of the brain to work on abstract problems.

 Women spread out their thinking over a wider area of the brain and tend to process more by integrating both hemispheres of the brain. Both men and women have similar rates of accuracy in problem solving, and giftedness seems to be distributed equally between the sexes.

THE DIFFERENT LEARNING STYLES OF BOYS AND GIRLS

It doesn't take much time teaching in the classroom to conclude that boys and girls learn differently. Neurotransmitters, essential parts of brain function that help to transmit messages in the brain, differ between boys and girls, resulting in clear differences in how the male and female brains process information. Areas of the brain related to language, speech, processing grammatical structures, and word production tend to be more developed or more highly active in girls, resulting in their improved verbal communications skills. Because boys mature in language centers later, they are two times as likely as girls to be diagnosed with learning disabilities and twice as likely to be placed in special education classes. While male students tend to use the right side of the brain to work on abstract problems, girls are able to access both hemispheres. Since the right side of the brain specializes in visual, spatial, and environmental awareness, as well as visual memory, boys tend to be superior at spatial relationships. Girls are able to take in more sensory data, so they are able to hear better; teachers may need a louder voice to reach boys. In early elementary school, boys are slower to master reading, but they are better at general math and three-dimensional reasoning. Later in elementary school, girls are generally better at fine motor skills and learning language. At the same time, boys are generally better at reading maps, and they will usually solve math problems without talking. Boys tend to be more interested in *finishing* an assignment while girls are more likely to be engaged in the *process* involved and working with others.

SOME CLASSROOM EXAMPLES

Gil Brown, a fifth-grade teacher at Mariposa Elementary School, provided a unique opportunity for his students to understand how girls and boys learn differently. He divided his students into groups of four, all of the same gender so that there were boy groups and girl groups. He gave each group a cardboard file box to assemble, the kind you can buy at office supply stores. To assemble the boxes, it's necessary to follow the printed directions. Within minutes, several of the boy groups announced that they were finished. However, none had properly assembled the boxes. The teacher told them to go back and check the directions. One of the boys even asked the teacher for duct tape, saying he could fix the box with tape. As I observed this activity, I was fascinated that the boys' approach, in many cases, was to modify the design rather than to follow the directions. The girl groups, on the other hand, took longer to complete the assignment but the boxes were assembled correctly and according to the directions. At least in this class, the girls read the directions, and the boys wanted to figure it out on their own. This lesson reinforced for me the notion that boys often just want to be done with a task, while girls enjoy the process.

Two sixth-grade teachers from Redlands Unified School District (USD), Anny Taylor and Marsha MacLean, once conducted an experiment as part of their master's degree program. Their project involved separating their students by gender and instructing them accordingly. Each teacher taught both groups throughout the day, presenting the same information but in different ways, according to brain research. The results were quite interesting. Both groups improved in their achievement when taught separately and issues related to deportment were reduced overall. There is current research on this topic which has prompted a resurgence of interest in separating the sexes for instruction.

SIX COMPONENTS OF BRAIN-COMPATIBLE LEARNING

The final pages of this chapter address six aspects of brain-compatible learning that can have a strong impact on classroom instruction. Teachers are encouraged to share this information, not just with their colleagues, but with their students as well.

BRAIN FOOD

Water is the most important *brain food.* Not only does it hydrate the body, but it provides oxygen to the brain and helps wash away the impurities in our diet. Students at my school were expected to bring water bottles to school every day, keeping them at their desks so that they would drink water throughout the day. Rather than raising their hands when they were thirsty, they simply drank from their water bottles which were close at hand.

This leads us to a discussion about brain food. Complex carbohydrates found in fruits, vegetables, and grains have been proven to enhance brain function. The *Caveman Diet* makes healthy eating easy for students to understand. Simply put, the *Caveman Diet* consists of food that is natural and nonprocessed, just like it's found in nature. Another way to promote healthy eating is by encouraging students to eat foods displayed around the perimeter of the supermarket, avoiding the aisles. Next time you go to the market, check out which foods are displayed around the store's perimeter, usually fresh vegetables and fruits; meat, fish, and poultry; bread and dairy. Then, notice which foods are found in the aisles, often processed foods, canned goods, and snacks, all loaded with preservatives and other additives. Since the brain is composed predominately of fat, similar to fish oil, the consumption of fish is excellent for the brain. Remember when we were told that fish was brain food? Well, it is!

When I was a principal, I used to go around the cafeteria at lunch time and inspect what students brought in their lunches. I would remind them about healthful eating habits, pointing out brain food as opposed to nonnutritional items. One of my favorite facts to share is that the icing on cupcakes, which parents often brought in to celebrate a child's birthday, was basically lard and sugar. When students realized that they were eating sweetened Crisco, they often turned up their noses at these so-called treats. Also, teachers who used food with their classes, as an incentive or reward, were encouraged to feature popcorn and nuts over candy. As educators, we should be concerned about the rise in childhood obesity. While we can't control what kids eat, we certainly can educate them about healthy eating. Helping them understand which foods are healthy and can help make them smarter might have the same result as our emphasis on the serious health issues connected to smoking. Americans today smoke significantly less than a generation ago and education has been partly responsible for this change. So, perhaps an emphasis on eating brain food might do the same toward improving health for the next generation.

FASTER PACE

The second big idea of *brain compatible classrooms* is the notion of *pacing*. Studies in the late 1990s used magnetic imaging to monitor brain activity. By studying changes in infrared light to gauge blood flow in the brain, researchers have been able to determine what part of the brain is firing during specific activities. Studies have uncovered the startling fact that a child's brain is *least active* while sitting in the classroom. However, two *spikes* in brain activity occur for students during the school day—at recess and lunchtime! This finding should raise an alarm for teachers. However, there are remedies. Just read on.

So, how do we encourage *active learning?* One suggestion is to *pick up the pace.* Harmin (2006) suggests a rather bold approach, which has been used successfully by hundreds of teachers. When one-third of the students have finished an assignment, he suggests that teachers pick up the papers and *move on to the next activity.* First, the teacher can announce, "Just a moment or two more." By using the word *moment* and not minute, students aren't prompted to look up from their work to check the clock. Within less than a minute, usually a third more of the students will finish and, within another few seconds, most will be done. I suggest that teachers follow this procedure with students four times in succession. Most students will become used to a faster pace within a short time. Now, I'm not going to lie to you and say that everyone will finish. After all, there are students who won't finish if you waited until the cows come home. However, this approach keeps the pace moving and prompts students to get started with assignments more quickly.

Another *pacing strategy* I encourage teachers to try is *underexplaining* assignments. As teachers, we tend to talk too much. Try telling students quickly what they need to do, and then let them get started. Not everyone has to listen to the many questions that students ask before they start an activity. Giving procedural directions only once has a strong impact on motivating students to listen the first time. "Turn to page 123 in your Social Studies textbook," frequently is followed by, "What page?" "What book?" Teachers often repeat these directions two or three times. Next time, try not responding. The more we teachers answer these types of questions, the more we inadvertently train students not to listen the first time. Students soon will learn that directions are given only once. Teachers might also accompany their nonresponse with what I call *The Look.* You know the one—it's a stare of total astonishment that someone has not paid attention. Students quickly learn to ask a table partner or look around before asking the teacher to repeat. Next time, these same students might listen the first time. Remember, this technique is effective when used to give *procedural* directions but should not be used when giving directions related to *content.* Questions like, "How do I work this long division problem?" might necessitate multiple explanations and actually are a major part of what we teachers do for a living.

MUSIC

Music is a third component of *brain-based learning.* Studies have shown that learning to play a musical instrument helps the brain process mathematics. Teachers should encourage students to take music lessons. Studies point to the fact that any musical instruction that requires students to learn music notation will make kids smarter, which even applies to voice lessons. Teachers also might consider playing music in their classrooms. As a principal, I played classical music over the public address system each morning for an hour before school so that students heard calming music as they walked onto the campus and while they were on the playground. Playing music helped reduce altercations on the playground and served as a tranquil way for students to start the day. Imagine walking onto the school grounds at 7:30 a.m. with Mozart pouring over you! Music became such an important part in the lives of our Mariposa students that we designated a different composer for each month of school. Each class was provided with a CD of that composer's music and a short biography which teachers used with their students.

Students at Mariposa School responded well to the following composers: Mozart, Handel, Beethoven, Vivaldi, Pachibel, and Bach. However, we also played ethnic music from various cultures as well as modern composers. The only music we didn't play were pieces that had lyrics. Lyrics tend to give the brain a mixed message. What we know about the neurological benefit of music is that it's about *patterns.* Since classical music is based on *patterns and repetition,* it appeals to the brain, which is a pattern-seeking organ.

Studies conducted at Brigham Young University (BYU) suggest that music can be played when students are writing, practicing math problems, during art, and for opening classroom exercises. The research cautions teachers, however, about playing music during silent reading or when directions are being given. While many students respond well to background music during reading, others aren't able to concentrate, so my suggestion is, *don't play music during reading.* The BYU research supports the premise that classical music enhances learning while also uplifting the soul. While the *Mozart Effect,* popular in the 1990s, may not have proven to be the neurological panacea to increase learning, it certainly won't do children any harm.

A final word needs to be said about *cultural literacy* and also *dignity.* School ought to be a place where cultural literacy is encouraged. Knowing the works of great composers, artists, and authors is part of developing cultural literacy. I believe that school should be a place of dignity, where students are exposed only to the finest works which then serve as examples for them to develop their own tastes and preferences. Children have enough time on their own to listen to other kinds of music at home; therefore, I don't think it's necessary to use school time for this purpose.

ROOM ENVIRONMENT

In a *brain-based classroom,* the teacher should remember that *whoever does the work gets smarter.* This concept applies to *room environment,* a fourth component of *brain-based learning.* Therefore, an important question for a teacher to ask frequently is, "Am I the one who needs to do this, or can my students do it?" When I visited an eighth-grade science class in Moreno Valley USD on the first day of school, I noticed that the walls were bare—there was absolutely no room environment put up by the teacher. However, at the beginning of each class period, the teacher gave students half sheets of poster board and assigned each of them a different element of the Periodic Table. The assignment was to create a poster listing the assigned element and its symbol, describing the element, and providing a picture showing how it might be used. For example, lithium might have a picture of a battery found in a camera or a prescription and a picture of a person with bipolar disorder (remember these were eighth graders!). By the end of the class period, each student had created a poster which was color-coded to correspond to the periodic table. By the end of that day, with the participation of five class periods, students had created posters for all 117 of the elements on the periodic table. After organizing and posting their work in the correct order, students had created an appropriate learning environment for the first trimester and *they also got smarter!* Not only did the teacher follow the precept that the kids should do the work, but he also followed the second element of a *brain-based* room environment: *every visual must in some way relate to the content.* No frivolous posters or cute bulletin boards were used and, most important, students were engaged in a meaningful assignment beginning the first day of class.

Another important consideration for a room environment that enhances *brain-compatible learning* is *displaying vocabulary* related to curriculum content. However, rather than the teacher printing the words, have the students do it. *Remember, whoever does the work gets smarter.*

One practice that doesn't seem to have much return for the effort is having good work boards, especially if the work consists of projects where everyone's paper looks alike. This doesn't mean you should refrain from displaying student work on the walls; it just means that kids probably won't learn from it, it's just wallpaper, so to speak. If you want kids to learn from each others' work, then feature the work in sample lessons. Teachers can use the overhead projector or distribute copies of student examples so everyone can benefit from seeing a good model.

Hart (1983) refers to the classroom rather cynically, as *a gentle prison.* He suggests that we *trap* our students in this gentle prison by surrounding them with visuals related to class content so that everything students see teaches something. In this way, when their attention strays from us, *and you know it will,* there will be something to catch their eyes, and they just might learn something. He suggests pulling down classroom maps so they are always visible. It is natural for students to look at maps and try to figure things out: *Which is my state? Where do my grandparents live? How far away is Disneyland?*

ATTENTION SPAN

No matter how interesting we think we are as teachers, the attention span of students seems pretty short. A fifth component of *brain-based learning* is *attention span*. In his research on how the brains of children work, Jensen (1998) explains this lack of attention from a *neurological* point of view. He contends that, when the brain is not actively involved in some learning activity, it tends to *turn off.* It's as if it is saying, "Since you aren't going to need me for anything important right now, I'll just take a little snooze." This is why creating frequent opportunities for *student output,* such as talking, writing, or making something, is so critical. Jensen offers a formula for anticipating a child's attention span: *Add three minutes to the age of the student and that's about how long he or she can sit still with no output activity.* So, if you are a second-grade teacher working with seven- and eight-year-olds, just add three to their ages and you will see that you have about 10 minutes of talking time before you lose them. For middle school students, it's about 15 minutes; for older students and most adults, their *attention span* is about 20 minutes.

So, with this information, how do we extend the attention spans of our students? The answer is threefold: The first choice is to create an *output activity* so that students can become more *actively engaged.* Harmin (2006) describes many appropriate output activities. A second option is to *change the matrix.* This simply means that the teacher can change what students see, their *matrix,* by moving around the room and teaching from different vantage points.

A third strategy comes from Jensen, who suggests *brain breaks* or *cross-laterals.* These simple movements, such as hugging yourself tightly, involve crossing the midline of the brain which *wakes up* the slumbering hemisphere. Other brain breaks include folding and unfolding your hands, then refolding them again with the opposite thumb on top. Do this about three or four times, each time alternating which thumb is on top. Another exercise is to pinch your nose with your left hand, while pulling your left ear with your right hand; then switch—your right hand goes to your nose, and your left hand goes to your right ear. It's sort of like patting your head and rubbing your stomach at the same time, then reversing. Brain breaks really help children stay focused, especially during tests when there often are no scheduled breaks. Another brain break you might try is having kids stand up to do their writing; more blood flows to the brain while standing. A goal for each teacher is to help your students understand their own physiology so that they can take *brain breaks* when they feel the need. Kids should perform *brain breaks* when their teacher begins to sound like Charlie Brown's teacher in the Peanuts cartoons. Remember the squawking? Unfortunately, that's sort of how we sound to students when their attention span is waning. Also, *don't forget the water!* If kids have water bottles on their desks, they always can take a drink and this also will help pump some valuable oxygen to their brains.

STRESS AND FEAR

The cognitive functions of the brain are located in the outer quarter-inch of the *cerebral cortex*. The rest of the cortex is predominately the fight/flight limbic part of the brain that is reactive to stimulus. When students are stressed repeatedly or when fearful, they retreat to the limbic brain. So, *stress and fear* are a sixth component of *brain-based learning.* If a student is riddled with anxiety, then no learning takes place. *The Master Teacher,* an educational publication, offers a pamphlet entitled *The Four Fears,* which provides useful explanations.

Fear of Loneliness

Everyone needs a friend. What about those students who have no one to play with at recess? Often, gifted youngsters prefer to stay in the classroom with their teacher. However, many teachers want them to go outside and socialize. Little do they realize that these students *are socializing,* with the one person who is most like them—*you!* If it's their preference, why not let them stay and talk with you? Being lonely is a real fear that causes students to retreat into themselves and prevents learning.

Fear of Looking Stupid

No one wants to appear foolish. Sometimes raising a hand to answer a question makes students feel stupid because of the reaction of peers. Middle school students often look at each other before answering the teacher's question, checking to see if it's okay to respond. *Intellectual bullying* is a way to make smart kids feel stupid. Sometimes kids won't even try to answer a question for fear of classmates laughing or ridiculing them. Intellectual bullying should not be tolerated and we teachers must send this strong message to offenders.

Fear of Failure

Nobody wants to fail. Failure is a common fear of our brightest youngsters who often are reluctant to try new challenges for fear of doing it *wrong.* Open-ended questions or creative tasks can be a *source of fear* for students who are used to being the best at everything. Sometimes our brightest youngsters are afraid to try new things for fear of doing them poorly. Teachers, who are willing to share personal experiences where they made mistakes, can help students see that making a mistake *isn't the end of the world.*

(Continued)

(Continued)

Fear of Embarrassment

Students need our love and respect, especially at times when they least deserve it. Disruptive students should not be reprimanded in front of the class. When we teachers embarrass a student in front of others, the student is humiliated and becomes resentful. Not only is learning turned off, the student is angry with us. Instead, we should speak to the student privately, without raising our voices. *Cynicism* and *sarcasm* are to be avoided when speaking to students because the brain has a difficult time processing this form of humor and may interpret comments literally. Do keep in mind, we need *three positives* before we can handle a *corrective,* so remind students repeatedly why they are such great kids.

SOME FINAL THOUGHTS

Now that we've looked at ways to make our classrooms more compatible with how the brain learns, it's time to investigate how to provide a curriculum that allows students to extend their thinking. In the next chapter, we examine the four components of a differentiated curriculum and strategies teachers can use to help *make all kids smarter.*

3 The Four Components of Differentiation

INTRODUCTION

The term *differentiated curriculum* has been so overused lately, that teachers frequently are told that the answer to the daunting problem of teaching to a wide range of ability levels and languages in the classroom is simply *to differentiate!* How easy does that sound? Well, it's not that easy, at least it wasn't for me. The term *differentiation* has become a *buzz word,* similar to *high expectations,* a term that filled articles and lectures for educators in the 1980s and 1990s. Authors define differentiation in different ways for various audiences. Sometimes differentiation is associated with *individualized instruction,* a focus of education in the 1970s.

For the purposes of this book, the terms *differentiation* or *differentiated curriculum* relate to the four components outlined by the National Association for Gifted Children (NAGC) and the California Association for the Gifted (CAG) in their position papers, as applied to the requirements for differentiating the curriculum specific to gifted and talented students. The intent, however, is not to provide high ability and gifted students with a *different* curriculum. What needs to be *different* are the *strategies* and *approaches* teachers use to help students reach and exceed the core standards. It also is a logical extension to assume that, if we apply these principles to a broader group of students, more students will have the opportunity to become smarter.

DEFINITION OF CURRICULUM DIFFERENTIATION

According to Kaplan and Gould (1999), " . . . a classroom where learners are provided with equal opportunity to learn, but are not expected to learn the same curriculum in the same way at the same time is the context that exemplifies differentiation" (p. 6). *Curriculum differentiation* is a broad term which encompasses the need to tailor instructional environments and practices to create appropriately different learning experiences for students with different needs.

Kathryn Keirouz (1993) suggests specific procedures to be used when differentiating curriculum for gifted and talented students, which include the following:

- Deleting already mastered material from existing curriculum
- Adding new content, process, or product expectations to existing curriculum
- Extending existing curriculum to provide enrichment activities
- Providing course work for able students at an earlier age than usual
- Writing new units or courses that meet the needs of gifted students

As explained in Barbara Clark's book, *Meeting the Challenge: A Guidebook for Teaching Gifted Students* (1996), published by CAG, there are four components of a differentiated curriculum. The four areas of differentiation are *acceleration and pacing*, *depth*, *complexity*, and *novelty*.

THE FOUR COMPONENTS OF A DIFFERENTIATED CURRICULUM

Acceleration and Pacing

Moving faster through the curriculum is an example of differentiated *pacing*. When a third of the students are done, move on! *Acceleration* allows students 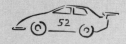 credit for what they know already and lets them move ahead. Don't have them repeat or review unnecessarily. Underexplain assignments; let students help one another. Give procedural directions ONCE! Keep moving at a fast pace, which is especially essential in mathematics.

Depth

 *Depth* is defined as becoming an expert in an area of study. It is the part of the curriculum that encourages students to learn more about a topic that might be introduced in the text or a lesson. Students explore outside

scholar or expert in the area of study. Students who study a topic in depth begin to think like a disciplinarian in their field.

Complexity

Finding the interrelatedness of content, how topics and ideas are connected or related to one another, is *complexity*. When students are given an opportunity to see how the content of their science unit relates to what they are studying in social studies or literature, they are being asked to think complexly. Complexity cannot exist without depth.

In order to relate content within or between disciplines, students need to know a lot about the content.

Novelty

 Novelty is the creative component of differentiation. It is the students and not the teachers who are the focus of novelty. Teachers who encourage novelty expect their students to demonstrate uniqueness in their work: *"Don't follow where the path leads, go where there is no path and leave a trail."* When teachers *underexplain* assignments, students are encouraged to stretch their wings through projects and products that are unique and original.

June Maker's model of differentiated curriculum (Maker 1982a, 1982b, 1986) explains how the curriculum should be differentiated in terms of the following:

- Learning environment
- Content modification
- Process modification
- Product modification

The charts below outline the way in which I have integrated the *CAG* and *Maker* models:

LEARNING ENVIRONMENT

The goal is to create a *learning environment* which encourages students to engage their abilities to the greatest extent possible, including taking risks and building knowledge and skills in what they perceive as a safe, flexible environment. Refer to the strategies outlined in Chapter 2 about the brain to see what

(Continued)

(Continued)

can be done in a learning environment that validates how the brain learns. This kind of learning environment has the following attributes:

- **Student centered**—focusing on the student's interests, input, and ideas rather than those of the teacher [**novelty**]
- **Encouraging independence**—tolerating and encouraging student initiative [**novelty**]
- **Open**—permitting new people, materials, ideas, and things to enter and nonacademic and interdisciplinary connections to be made [**complexity, novelty**]
- **Accepting**—encouraging acceptance of ideas and opinions before evaluating them [**depth**]
- **Complex**—including a rich variety of resources, media, idea, methods, and tasks [**depth, complexity**]
- **Highly mobile**—encouraging movement in and out of groups, desk settings, classrooms, and schools [**acceleration and pacing**]

CONTENT MODIFICATION

The object of *content modification* is to remove the ceiling regarding what can be learned, using the abilities of students to build a richer and more diverse knowledge base. *Content modification* can be facilitated by encouraging the following:

- **Abstractness**—shifting content from facts, definitions, and descriptions to concepts, relationships, themes, and generalizations [**complexity**]
- **Complexity**—shifting content to interdisciplinary relationships rather than considering factors separately [**complexity**]
- **Variety**—expanding content beyond material presented in the normal program [**depth**]
- **Study of people**—including the study of individuals or groups of people and how they have reacted to various opportunities and problems [**depth**]
- **Study of methods of inquiry**—including procedures used by experts working in their fields [**depth**]

PROCESS MODIFICATION

The reason for *process modification* is to promote creativity and higher level cognitive skills, while encouraging productive use and management of the knowledge the students have mastered. *Process modification* can be assisted by encouraging the following:

- **Higher levels of thinking**—involving cognitive challenge using Bloom's Taxonomy of Cognitive Processes, logic problems, critical thinking, and problem solving [**complexity**]
- **Creative thinking**—regarding imagination, intuitive approaches, and brainstorming techniques [**novelty**]
- **Open-endedness**—encouraging risk-taking and inquiries that have multiple answers [**depth, complexity, novelty**]
- **Group interaction**—permitting highly able and motivated students to work together and to challenge each other's thinking [**pacing**]
- **Variable pacing**—allowing students to move through lower order thinking tasks more rapidly while allowing more time for students to respond fully for higher order thinking tasks [**pacing**]
- **Variety of learning experiences**—accommodating different learning styles of students and providing opportunities for them to make choices [**novelty**]
- **Debriefing**—encouraging students to be aware of and able to articulate their reasoning or conclusion to a problem or question [**depth**]
- **Freedom of choice**—allowing students to choose their projects, activities, and methods for demonstrating their knowledge [**novelty, complexity**]

PRODUCT MODIFICATION

The aim of *product modification* is to provide opportunities for talented students to produce products that reflect their interests and potential. *Product modification* can be supported by incorporating the following strategies:

- **Real problems**—providing students with relevant real-life problems and activities [**depth, novelty**]
- **Real audiences**—allowing students to have an audience that is appropriate for the product, such as another student or group of students, the classroom teacher, other teachers, an assembly, a community group, a mentor, or a specific interest group [**depth, complexity**]
- **Real deadlines**—encouraging students to use time management skills and realistic planning [**pacing**]
- **Transformations**—promoting original manipulation of information by students rather than regurgitation [**novelty**]
- **Appropriate evaluation**—allowing students to self- and peer-evaluate their projects using a predetermined rubric created by students or the teacher [**complexity**]

SOME STRATEGIES FOR DIFFERENTIATING THE CURRICULUM

In the following section, I have included some of my favorite games and activities to give teachers ideas for beginning the process of differentiating the curriculum. These activities are organized according to the *four components of differentiation.* Carolyn Callahan, Professor of Education at the University of Virginia, and noted author and expert on gifted education, offers some additional strategies for differentiating curriculum.

USING ACCELERATION AND PACING TO DIFFERENTIATE THE CURRICULUM

Acceleration and *pacing* are especially important in mathematics. Students who are advanced in math do not want to spend time reviewing and doing  problems that they already know how to do. It's a waste of their time. Teachers can start each math lesson by assessing prior knowledge in quick and nonthreatening ways. We have a tendency to test our students into *cognitive oblivion* (my term!). In schools today, in fact, students often are tested for the equivalent of one full month of school by the time you add up all of the district and state assessments. This amount of time spent on mandated assessments significantly decreases time devoted to student instruction. We don't want to increase further time spent on lengthy tests, but teachers do need to assess student knowledge on a regular basis. Therefore, I suggest we try some of the following quick and easy ways to check if students already have the concept mastered and are ready to move on:

USING *YES/NO* CARDS

All students have in front of them both a *green* and a *red* card, or a *yes* and *no* card. If they understand the concept presented and are ready to move on, they flash the teacher the *green* or the *yes* card. If they don't understand or are unsure, they flash the *red* or the *no* card.

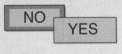

CREATE A WEB

If students can create a web demonstrating their understanding of the concept, they probably know a lot about it. Having students create a diagram of the concept helps them and the teacher see if they understand it. This technique is described further in Chapter 10, under note-taking strategies.

FIST TO FIVE

How much understanding do students have about a concept or procedure? Have them each hold one hand in front of their chests and show you. A fist indicates no understanding (*I don't have a clue what you're talking about*), one to two fingers  mean some understanding (*I know a little*), and five fingers signifies a great deal of understanding (*Stand aside teacher; I can teach this lesson to the class as well as you can!*).

Because students aren't holding up their hands, they are able to quietly and privately share their level of understanding with the teacher. If there are mostly three, four, and five fingers, that's an indication the teacher can move on. However, if there are lots of fists and one to two fingers, it might be time to gather the troops for a quick reteach. But, keep in mind, there is nothing that says that everyone has to go through the reteaching lesson, only those who need it.

DO THE FIVE HARDEST

The teacher asks if students wish to *challenge* the chapter and *test out* of it. This strategy works most effectively in mathematics. Those who want to try are given the five hardest problems to do in class. (The teacher selects the problems from the test at the end of the chapter. At least two of the five problems should be in the form of a *story* problem.) Students who get at least four out of five problems correct don't need to do that chapter and can move into the *Math Masters* group.

The *Math Masters* group works on supplemental material. Although they may move ahead in the text, usually they go into more *depth* within the content area. For example, if the class is learning how to multiply five-digit numbers by two-digit numbers, the *Math Masters* group might practice multiplying eight-digit numbers by six-digit numbers. These students should not be required to do the regular class assignments or homework for that chapter. Any homework they are assigned should be related to what they are doing, not what the rest of the class is doing.

PLATOONING

 This strategy is a modification of team teaching in which the entire grade-level staff agrees to teach math at the same time. Top students from all classes at that grade level are identified, according to test scores, and then *grouped together* for math instruction. All other students, who are average and below in math, are divided into *heterogeneous groups*. (While there is a great deal of research to support the practice of placing high-ability students together for math instruction, research does not support doing the same with low ability students.)

USING DEPTH TO DIFFERENTIATE THE CURRICULUM

 Activities that encourage *depth* of learning provide students with opportunities to learn more about the content than is usually presented in the text, often allowing them to become experts in the vocabulary relating to the content. A strategy that I have used in my seminars with great success is what I call *Language of the Discipline* cards.

MAKING LANGUAGE OF THE DISCIPLINE CARDS

Flashcards are made by cutting colored 3 x 5 index cards in half. Cards are color-coded by subject, for example, green for science, yellow for math, and so forth. As students come across **boldfaced** vocabulary in their texts, they write those words on flash cards. As they gain familiarity with content vocabulary, students progress to creating their own *working definition* of each word and writing it on the back of the appropriate flashcard. (Students should *not* just copy definitions from the glossary as they don't learn as much.) Each student's set of color-coded cards can be stored in a ziplock bag and kept in her desk for quick review before recess, right after lunch, or whenever there are a few spare minutes.

By the time the year is over, each student will have a very large set of personal vocabulary cards. You will be surprised that just 5 to 10 minutes of daily review will significantly increase vocabulary and understanding of content. The games which follow provide additional opportunities for students to work in pairs or triads to increase vocabulary and understanding of content.

PASSWORD

One student draws a card from his bag and gives his partner a synonym or single word that might lead his partner to say the word on the card. (No part of the word itself may be used as a clue.) The partner makes a guess. If incorrect, the first student then gives a second one-word clue. Play continues until the word is guessed correctly; then the turn passes to the partner.

   With this game, I have found that pairs work best. This game benefits both students because, while one is sharing *inductively*, the other is responding *deductively*. Both are getting smarter.

Here is a sample dialog of a password game based upon the word *peninsula*:

Student A: *geography*

Student B: *map*

Student A: *landform*

Student B: *mountain*

Student A: *Florida*

Student B: *swamp*

Student A: *Italy*

Student B: **peninsula**

Student A: "You are correct!"

KEEP ON TALKING

This is a variation of *Password* except that, instead of sharing one-word clues, each student, in turn, keeps on talking about the term until her partner correctly guesses it. Players speak in complete sentences, providing as much information as fast as they can, until their partner figures out the term. This game can be played in pairs or in triads where one student is providing clues and the other two are guessing.

Here is a sample scenario:

Student A: "This is a landform where water surrounds the land on three sides. Florida is an example of this landform and so is Italy. It's not an island because part of the land juts out into the water and the rest is connected to the mainland."

Student B: "Peninsula?"

Student A: "Whew! It's about time! I was running out of things to say!"

KNOW AND *DON'T KNOW* PILES

Students take their pack of cards and sort them into two piles: the words they *know* and the words they *don't know*. Once sorted, they take three cards from the *don't know* pile and go around the room to find the answer from a fellow student. Some teachers have added a third pile: *know a little*.

OTHER STRATEGIES THAT ENCOURAGE DEPTH

In addition to the games I've described, here are some additional strategies teachers can use to help students increase their *depth* of understanding. These strategies are explained in the box that follows:

STRATEGIES FOR INCREASING DEPTH

- **Allow students to solve as many of their own daily social problems as possible.** A teacher at my school once said to a student who was tattling, "Is there blood?" If not, my assumption is that the students probably have the ability to solve the problem without the "divine intervention" of their teacher. The more we ask students to solve their own problems the better.
- *Underexplain* **the content or assignment instead of giving too many details.** This doesn't mean that teachers quit explaining. It does mean that teachers allow the students who don't need yet another example or another repeat of the instructions to go on and get started.
- **Expect students to defend what they say.** Using Socratic dialogs, presented in detail in Chapter 8, is an excellent strategy for requiring students to be held accountable for what comes out of their mouths. We should expect them to defend what they say with evidence and to define what they mean by the words they are using. More about this later.

USING COMPLEXITY TO DIFFERENTIATE THE CURRICULUM

The more we tell students what is important to us, the less we will know what is important to them. When expecting students to think *complexly*, we are asking them to *relate content to ideas.* If we *tell* them the *Big Idea*, we are effectively robbing them of making the connections themselves. Asking the students complex questions does not mean that the teacher already has an answer in his head. When I make the connection in my head first, I find that I tend to ask leading questions and the students spend their time trying to second-guess me. What if I asked them to make a connection between two content pieces and I haven't a clue what that connection might be? This is a better strategy for students because they are more likely to be actively involved in real-life questions.

Consider a spelling assignment, for example, where the teacher asks students to take their spelling words and sort them into the parts of speech. Although this isn't a complex activity, it is an effective way to check for comprehension and knowledge of grammar. However, what if the teacher said, "Go home tonight, take your spelling words and sort them into three groups. The immediate response from students might be, "What groups do you want?" The teacher can respond by saying, "If I knew that, then I wouldn't have asked you. Come back tomorrow with your spelling words sorted into three groups and explain to me how you sorted them." This is an example of allowing students to think *complexly*. By *underexplaining* the assignment, the teacher put the burden of thinking on the shoulders of the students. Remember, *whoever does the work gets smarter*.

Remember the *Language of the Discipline* cards from the previous section on depth? As an activity to have students think complexly, why not use the cards to play a game sort of like dominoes? I call this activity *Think Links*.

THINK LINKS

Each player is dealt five cards from her own bag of vocabulary cards; the rest are placed face down in a pile. The top card is turned over.

Students take turns trying to make a *Think Link* between the top card and one from their hand. For example, a student might lay down a card that says: The students might decide that *Napoleon* and *peninsula* can be linked because they both stick out from the group. A *peninsula* sticks out from the land like *Napoleon* stuck out from the rest of European leaders.

| Peninsula |
| Napoleon |

There are many links, some simple, others more complex. A student might have said that *Napoleon* invaded Italy, which is a *peninsula*. That would work too. So would the fact that both are nouns. The next player tries to make a link from either *Napoleon* or *peninsula*, kind of like dominoes. If a player can't make a link, he can draw another card from the pile and make a link from that card. Or better yet, have students make up their own rules. This game was made up by a student of mine. He should have patented it!

AUTHENTIC PROJECTS

Authentic projects probably are the most complex activities for students. Projects are representative of performance in a professional field, allowing us to evaluate performance against a model or standard. Self-assessment of a project plays a key role for our gifted students. Since projects incorporate a variety of skills, they integrate many brain activities. However, writing should be a part of *every* project students complete. Projects also should require *sustained work*. There is more about projects in Chapter 10.

USING NOVELTY TO DIFFERENTIATE THE CURRICULUM

As a principal, I recall a particular situation when I was scheduled to observe a reading lesson in a first-grade classroom. I settled myself at the back of the classroom, clipboard in hand, waiting for what I expected to be a well-executed and highly predicable lesson using the reading anthology. However, just before the lesson was to begin, one of the students raised his hand and asked the teacher if he could share what had happened to him at the dentist the day before. I expected the teacher to ask the student to wait until after the lesson. Instead, she handed the six-year-old a white-board and some dry-erase markers and said, "Kevin, knock yourself out!" To my astonishment and elation, this little guy got up and drew a diagram of a mouth, labeled the teeth, and proceeded to give what I consider to be one of the best lectures on dental hygiene. He even answered questions from the class, admonishing those who asked redundant questions: "Pay attention; I've already answered that question!"

Now where was the *novelty* in this lesson? It happened when the teacher decided that this student had something worthy to share. The teacher did not *provide* the novelty, she *permitted* it to happen. Of course, I can hear you saying, "Now everyone's going to want to share and there isn't time for that." You're right, but this teacher handled it expertly. She told the class that she would like to hear about their experiences, but that the principal was here to observe a lesson. Instead, she invited them to share their stories with her during recess. Of course, by the time recess rolled around, no one remembered, but I'm sure she would have stayed in to listen if they had reminded her.

ADDRESSING NOVELTY THROUGH PROJECTS

Novelty also can be expressed through projects. A project should be rich in curricular content, related to the performance standards of the grade level, and also reflect something in its design about the student who created it. Teachers can help students create appropriate projects by guiding them away from those that do not cover enough of the performance standards or do not increase their depth of understanding content. Just because a student wants to do a particular project, teachers should give the *go-ahead* only to those projects that meet these criteria. Remember, in the business world, many projects die for lack of approval.

Another thought regarding projects is that the more teachers explain the details of the assignment, the less *novelty* is involved for the students. A high school teacher friend of mine, Jim Satterfield, assigns what he calls a *knock my socks off* project for the end of the year. Students choose a content-related topic from the curriculum, which in this case is American history, and attempt to use *originality* and *creativity* in their projects, to present important and accurate information that enriches their own understanding. In this example, *novelty* is addressed in the presentation of content-related material.

SOME FINAL THOUGHTS

Now, hold up your fingers. A fist means I've confused you completely; five fingers indicate you are more than ready to proceed. If you don't thoroughly understand *differentiated curriculum* yet, fear not! The rest of this book contains more instructional strategies to get you and your students thinking about the four components of a differentiated curriculum: *acceleration and pacing, depth, complexity,* and *novelty.* I've got a lot of ideas and strategies left to share with you. *We've only just begun . . . .*

4 Interdisciplinary Thematic Instruction

INTRODUCTION

In this chapter you will learn how to incorporate a year-long, *interdisciplinary theme* to increase *depth* and *complexity* in your teaching. The concept of *interdisciplinary thematic instruction* owes much to the work of philosopher, educator, and author, Mortimer Adler, who compiled a set of reference books entitled *Great Books of the Western World* (1952a). This set, similar in number to an encyclopedia, is a collection of the works of Aristotle, Plato, Locke, Gibbon, Descartes, Cervantes, Freud, and Shakespeare, to name but a few. A supplemental two-volume set, which accompanies *Great Books,* is called *The Syntopicon: An Index to the Great Ideas* (1952b). *The Syntopicon,* used much like a thesaurus, cross-references the great themes or ideas of Western thought with actual works of the great thinkers. In other words, if you want to find out what Cervantes said about greed, you would look up *greed* in *The Syntopicon* to find all the annotated references in his works. Then, the specific references can be found in *Great Books* and read in their entirety.

Now, fast-forward a few decades from the 1950s, to the collaborative work of Sandra Kaplan and Barbara Clark. In the 1970s to 1980s, these noted authorities in gifted education introduced the concept of teaching with a *year-long theme,* which they referred to as *interdisciplinary thematic instruction,* because the same theme was addressed through reading, mathematics, science, and the other disciplines. Much like an umbrella, the theme is an overarching idea for addressing curriculum content throughout the year. All themes should be ideas or major concepts that can be tied to content, as illustrated in the chart that follows:

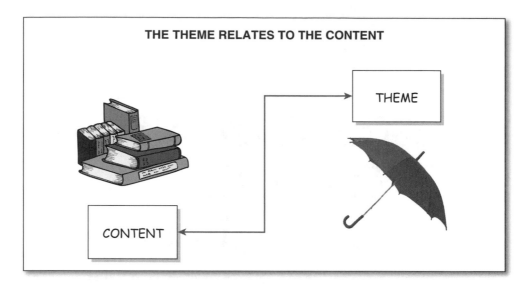

A YEAR-LONG THEME

The purpose of selecting a *year-long theme* is to help students *relate content in meaningful ways.* With this in mind, the theme should be broad enough to encompass various subject areas and disciplines. Whenever teachers ask students *how the content relates to the theme,* they are asking students to think *complexly.* In my seminars, I offer the following guidelines to help teachers select a year-long theme:

GUIDELINES FOR SELECTING A YEAR-LONG THEME

- The theme should be an idea the teacher understands.
- The theme should have some relevance to the content taught.
- The theme should be broad enough to cross over from one subject, or discipline, to another.
- The teacher should not be particularly concerned that the previous year's teacher had the same theme. Remember, the content changes.
- The theme forms an *umbrella* over the content.

Doctors Kaplan and Clark, as part of their work regarding *interdisciplinary thematic instruction,* have generated a list of themes which teachers may use as the focus for the entire school year. The following year, just for variety, the teacher might select a different theme. A list of possible year-long themes is shown in the chart that follows:

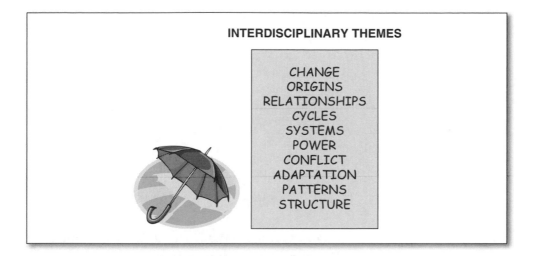

INTERDISCIPLINARY THEMES

CHANGE
ORIGINS
RELATIONSHIPS
CYCLES
SYSTEMS
POWER
CONFLICT
ADAPTATION
PATTERNS
STRUCTURE

SELECTING A YEAR-LONG THEME

As you think about *themes,* examine the previous list to determine which theme best suits your curriculum. Think broadly, *across the disciplines.* Avoid thinking exclusively about history/social science, or math, or English/language arts. However, if you are a single-subject teacher, then by all means think about your particular discipline. Does one of the themes seem more relevant because of its *connectivity?* Then, that's the one for you! If not, just pick one that seems interesting. Over the years, I have seen *thematic instruction* successfully incorporated into many gifted classes, as well as regular classrooms.

RELATING CONTENT TO THEME

Having a theme for your class provides an opportunity for teachers to ask questions in each subject area, on a daily basis, which are related to the theme. This practice encourages *complex thinking.* The following questions are examples:

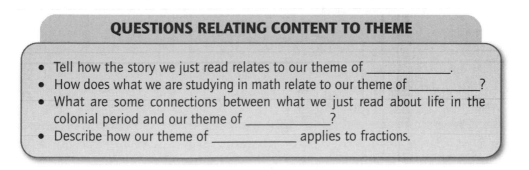

QUESTIONS RELATING CONTENT TO THEME

- Tell how the story we just read relates to our theme of _____.
- How does what we are studying in math relate to our theme of _____?
- What are some connections between what we just read about life in the colonial period and our theme of _____?
- Describe how our theme of _____ applies to fractions.

All of these questions are quite *complex*. However, as the teacher, you do *not* need to know the answers to any of these questions. *Let the students do the thinking!* Sometimes, when we have the answers in our heads already, we tend to look for those same answers when we question our students. Remember, we are trying to build *complex thinking patterns* in our students. Our desire is to make them smarter. Let them *chew* on these ideas, *wrestle* with them, *ponder* them. These are deep questions. *Relationary thinking is complex thinking.*

USING APHORISMS OR GENERALIZATIONS

Another piece to the teaching of themes is the use of *aphorisms*, which are *truisms* or *generalizations*. When added to the concept of *thematic instruction*, *aphorisms* form yet another layer of *depth* and *complexity*. Once students and teachers have generated a few *generalizations* or *aphorisms* related to the theme, the students then can determine which ones best apply to specific curriculum content. The next chart shows some examples of *aphorisms* used with a theme:

FOUR APHORISMS RELATED TO THE THEME OF *CHANGE*

- Change is inevitable.
- Change causes other things to change.
- Change can be fast or slow.
- Change can be natural or imposed.

ASKING STUDENTS TO USE APHORISMS

Once these *generalizations* or *aphorisms* are posted, students can be asked to identify the *change* in the content (i.e., story, event in history, scientific process, math problem, etc.) and then to determine which of the *aphorisms* best applies to the *change* stated. For example, a teacher might ask students to discuss the changes that need to take place in order for the subtraction problem to be completed correctly. A *deeper question* might be, "Which of the aphorisms above best applies to the *change* associated with regrouping when solving a subtraction problem?" While students might be able to make a case for each of the four aphorisms listed, the second one probably is most relevant. Here are some more examples of how to apply aphorisms to themes and content:

Which aphorisms apply when discussing the *changes* that took place in California during the **Gold Rush?** Can you make a case for each of them?

How did each of the following characters change in the novel, **Charlotte's Web?** Which aphorism best describes the changes that took place in each of the characters?

Fern

Wilbur

Templeton

Charlotte

RELATING APHORISMS TO A THEME

After examining these diagrams, select your theme and see if you can find *four generalizations* or *aphorisms* that are related to the theme. Then you can begin the process of introducing the class to the theme using a series of

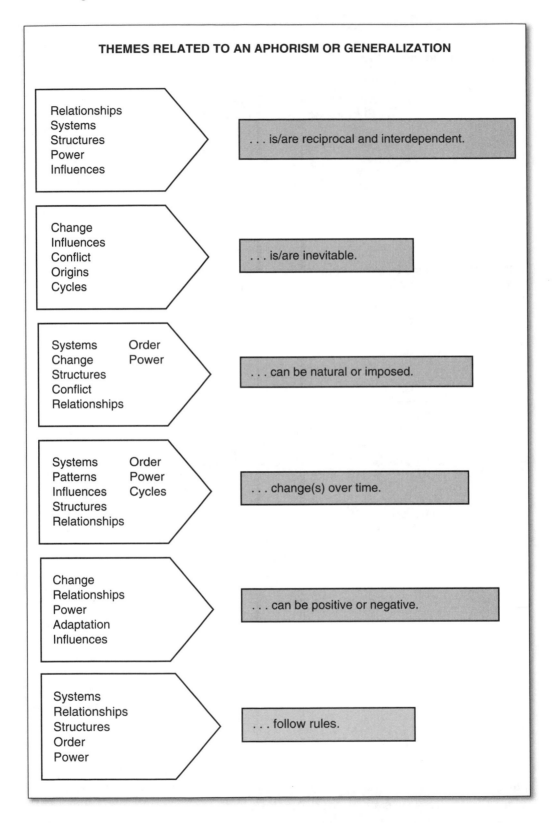

THEMES RELATED TO AN APHORISM OR GENERALIZATION

Relationships
Systems
Structures
Power
Influences

. . . is/are reciprocal and interdependent.

Change
Influences
Conflict
Origins
Cycles

. . . is/are inevitable.

Systems   Order
Change   Power
Structures
Conflict
Relationships

. . . can be natural or imposed.

Systems   Order
Patterns   Power
Influences   Cycles
Structures
Relationships

. . . change(s) over time.

Change
Relationships
Power
Adaptation
Influences

. . . can be positive or negative.

Systems
Relationships
Structures
Order
Power

. . . follow rules.

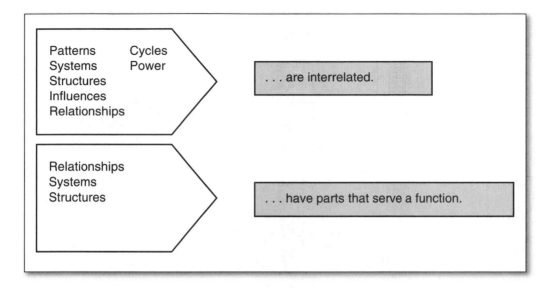

short lessons. I have seen teachers visually represent their year-long theme in a variety of ways. One teacher posted the theme above the whiteboard, showing the four aphorisms on either side with arrows pointing to the central theme:

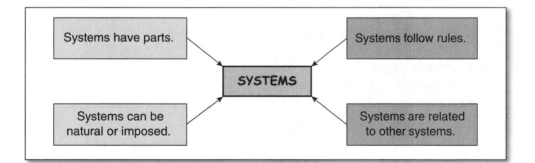

I have seen other teachers devote a bulletin board to the theme and then apply lessons to the board by adding sentence strips related to the topic at hand. Thus, *the content changes, but the aphorisms related to the theme always remain the same,* as seen in the following example related to the *circulatory system:*

Teachers also can relate the theme to a writing assignment. Making a thematic connection is a great topic for an essay. The following example shows how teachers might have students use *aphorisms* to demonstrate *understanding of a concept,* even in a testing situation:

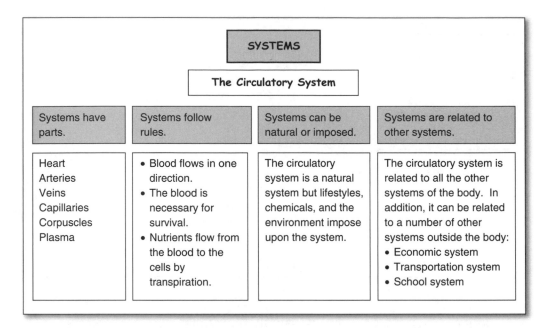

SYSTEMS			
The Circulatory System			
Systems have parts.	Systems follow rules.	Systems can be natural or imposed.	Systems are related to other systems.
Heart Arteries Veins Capillaries Corpuscles Plasma	• Blood flows in one direction. • The blood is necessary for survival. • Nutrients flow from the blood to the cells by transpiration.	The circulatory system is a natural system but lifestyles, chemicals, and the environment impose upon the system.	The circulatory system is related to all the other systems of the body. In addition, it can be related to a number of other systems outside the body: • Economic system • Transportation system • School system

We have just finished studying about the Middle Ages. Select one of the prompts listed and write about how it relates to the four generalizations that are posted in the front of the room:

- Discuss the *Feudal System* as it relates to the four generalizations of *systems.*
- Discuss the *system* of *Commerce and Trade Routes* as related to the four generalizations of *systems.*
- *The Church* was a powerful *system* during the *Middle Ages.* Discuss this *system* as it relates to the four generalizations.
- Discuss the *system* of *Chivalry* as it relates to the four generalizations.

PRESENTING THE CONCEPT OF A THEME

Teachers can present the concept of a *year-long theme* to students in a variety of ways, often depending upon the grade level of the class. Let's say the year-long theme is *relationships.* A teacher could ask, "What always is true about relationships?" After students share their ideas, the teacher might suggest some additional ideas. At the conclusion of discussion, there should be about *four aphorisms* or *generalizations* written on the board that *always are true* about relationships. Here is an example:

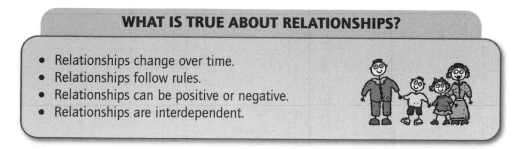

WHAT IS TRUE ABOUT RELATIONSHIPS?

- Relationships change over time.
- Relationships follow rules.
- Relationships can be positive or negative.
- Relationships are interdependent.

Next, students can analyze the *relationships* that they know the most about—their families. Each student might create a *graphic organizer* on a piece of blank paper, filling in the diagram with specific information about his own family. Students might draw pictures that illustrate the *connection* of *family* to the theme of *relationships.*

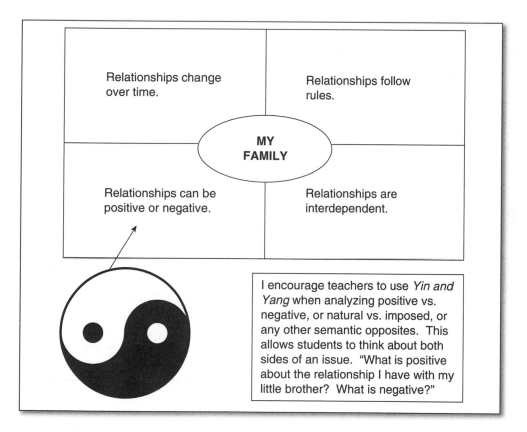

Relationships change over time.

Relationships follow rules.

MY FAMILY

Relationships can be positive or negative.

Relationships are interdependent.

I encourage teachers to use *Yin and Yang* when analyzing positive vs. negative, or natural vs. imposed, or any other semantic opposites. This allows students to think about both sides of an issue. "What is positive about the relationship I have with my little brother? What is negative?"

EXAMPLES FROM TEACHERS

Graphic organizers may be used by students either individually, as described in the previous example, or in small groups, or even with the whole class. For example, Margee Fuller used a graphic organizer to introduce the concept of *systems* to her fourth-grade class. Together, they examined the *school system* using the *four generalizations,* and they charted the following information:

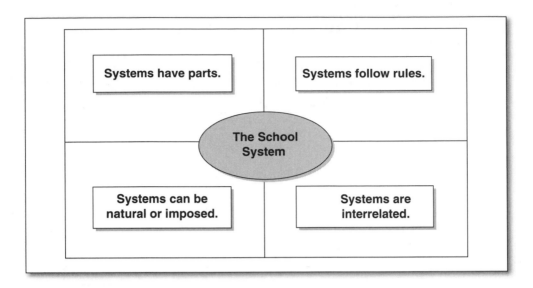

See if you can do it. List 10 *components* of the school system. Now, think of some rules that apply to the school system. Decide whether the school system is *natural or imposed*. If it's imposed, is there any part of the system that is natural? Consider *desire to learn* or *curiosity*. Finally, how does the school system relate to other systems?

In a middle school class, another teacher used *systems* as his theme and had students brainstorm all the *systems* they could think of, writing them on the board:

Sewer	Government	Computer	Dewey Decimal	Legal
Dating	Number	Money	Circulatory	Nervous
Muscle	Respiratory	Welfare	Criminal Justice	Transportation
Solar	School	Family	Equations	Electrical

Each pair of students then chose one system to analyze based upon the *four generalizations*. The final activity used the fourth aphorism: *Systems are interrelated.* Students created a link between each of the systems to show how they are related:

- The *sewer system* is related to the *government system* in that they both have a lot of waste in them.
- The *computer system* is related to the *Dewey Decimal System* in that they both use numbers to help organize data.
- The *legal system* is related to the *dating system* in that the dating system has laws related to conduct on a date.

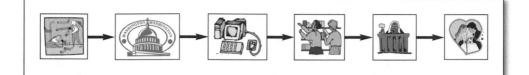

This type of activity not only is an exercise in *complexity,* but it is a fun and interesting *mental pursuit* that is engaging to high-ability students.

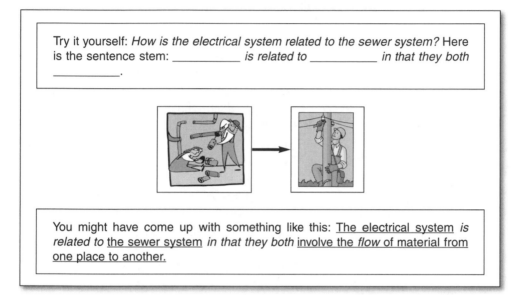

Try it yourself: *How is the electrical system related to the sewer system?* Here is the sentence stem: _____ *is related to* _____ *in that they both* _____.

You might have come up with something like this: The electrical system *is related to* the sewer system *in that they both* involve the *flow* of material from one place to another.

As teachers explore *interdisciplinary thematic instruction,* we should be aware of a few reminders, as well as cautions, which are described here:

SOME CAUTIONS
and
SOME REMINDERS

SOME CAUTIONS AND SOME REMINDERS

- When teaching with an interdisciplinary theme, the teacher needs to make some of the initial connections first, so that the students can hear them and discuss them. Don't expect students to see these relationships right away. They are not used to thinking this way and need a few examples to get them going.
- Connections aren't always between *literature* and *science,* or *history* and *literature,* or *art* and *mathematics.* Sometimes they are between the various disciplines *within* the area of study, for example, *sociology* and *anthropology, economics* and *history, biology* and *astronomy.*

- Caution: Try not to *trivialize* these connections. Once a teacher came to me very excited about her year-long theme: *Disneyland.* Each of the lands represented a different subject in school: Math = Main Street, Science = Tomorrowland, Geography = Adventureland, and so forth. I tried to explain that this is not *interdisciplinary thematic instruction,* even though Disneyland is a *theme* park. The core to interdisciplinary thematic instruction is the connecting of the *content* to an *idea,* not a tourist attraction. Start with the list of 10 themes presented in this chapter.
- Because the brain is wired to make *connections,* this style of teaching is *brain-compatible.* We're not asking students to do something that they can't do; it's just that they may not be used to thinking this way.
- Scripted teaching, where teachers are required to follow the teachers' guide, much like an actor follows a script, is *rote* teaching, the lowest level on *Bloom's Taxonomy.* Teachers should know the standards and the curriculum, but they should not be expected to follow a script to teach the content standards. Content standards can be taught in a wide variety of ways, depending upon the students and the talent of the teacher. Thematic teaching *extends* the content standards.
- *Projects* are an excellent way for students to *connect content to the theme.* For example, asking students to create a project that demonstrates the *changes* that have taken place in technology between two time periods is a way of *connecting the theme* (change) to more authentic tasks.
- *Collaboration* is an important aspect of *success in the workplace.* Having students work in pairs or triads to discuss and respond to thematic questions is an excellent way for them to learn the skills of *collaboration* and *collegiality.* Sometimes gifted and high-ability students would rather work alone. Working alone from *time to time* is not a problem; however, the world we live in is collaborative. We need to provide our students many opportunities to *work together* so they get used to it.

SOME FINAL THOUGHTS

As we progress through the remainder of this book, I will be referencing *interdisciplinary themes* in a variety of other ways. It is a strategy that incorporates both *depth and complexity.* Remember, whenever students are asked to relate the *content* they are learning to an *idea,* that is *complex thinking.* Teaching with a *year-long theme* allows students to think *complexly* on a regular basis. The *Icons of Depth and Complexity,* which are explained in the next chapter, work very well with *interdisciplinary thematic instruction* because both concepts are designed to *increase complex, in-depth thinking* so that it becomes a natural part of every lesson, every day.

5 The Icons of Depth and Complexity

INTRODUCTION

The *Icons of Depth and Complexity* are a series of *pictures* that represent the *elements of depth and complexity* as they relate to a *differentiated curriculum*. The *Icons of Depth and Complexity* were developed by Sandra Kaplan and Betty Gould with the *icon symbols* created by Sheila Madsen. The *Icons of Depth and Complexity* represent a major contribution to the lexicon of gifted education and to the bank of strategies which teachers can use with gifted youngsters, as well as students of all ability levels. Subsequently, many supplemental materials have been published related to the use of the *Icons of Depth and Complexity*. While these publications are available for purchase from a variety of sources, some free information and suggested activities can be found on the Internet, posted by teachers using the *Icons of Depth and Complexity,* so Google your hearts out! Another source, J. Taylor Education, allows free downloads of the *Icons of Depth and Complexity* from its website (http://www.jtayloreducation.com), and it also is the exclusive publisher of *Icon* cards, magnets, and other products related to *differentiating instruction*.

The *Icons of Depth and Complexity* are divided into two obvious groups: those related to *depth* and those pertaining to *complexity*. Remember, *depth* is defined as *becoming an expert in a field* and means knowing a lot about a topic. *Complexity* is the *interrelatedness of the content to other content*, within and between the various subjects and disciplines. When using the *icons,* as with any strategies we learn from others, I believe it's important for teachers to personalize them, to modify them, and to adapt them so that

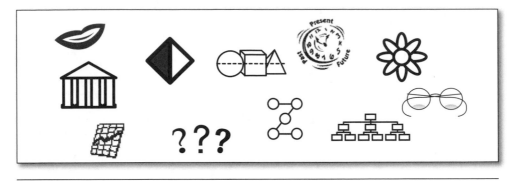

Used with permission, JTaylorEducation.com

they become an integral part of your teaching repertoire. This is what I have done and I encourage you to do the same.

THE ICONS OF DEPTH

In the pages which follow, I have described the ways in which I have used the *Icons of Depth* with students and also how I've explained them to teachers attending my seminars.

LANGUAGE OF THE DISCIPLINE

The *language of the discipline* icon represents the technical vocabulary associated with the content. These are the terms that are in **bold print** within the text, plus other words. These are the scholarly terms and also the jargon of the discipline. Think of all the jargon associated with *our* profession. Sometimes I get *acronym overload* (NCLB, NAGC, RSP, TAG, GATE, UGH!). When students see the *language of the discipline* icon, they know that they will be expected to *define the vocabulary* of the content they are studying. All *language of the discipline* words can be found within the text, *except* in English/language arts, where these terms are outside the text or the story. For instance, *plot, summary, voice, characterization, setting, climax, and conflict* are *language of the discipline* words, but they can't be found directly in the novel or anthology story. However, *examples* of these terms *can* be found within the story. The term *muggle* is used to describe nonwizard people in the Harry Potter books; however, it is not a *language of the discipline* word, but rather it is an example of *plot* and *setting*. Students will not find the word *metaphor* in a poem but should be able to find *examples* of metaphors when they look carefully. *Metaphor* is part of the *language of the discipline* for writing.

ETHICS

The icon for *ethics* asks students to consider issues of *right and wrong* related to the content. Teachers can pose an *ethical question* by asking students, "Is it right to . . . ?" Sometimes, however, these questions are rather one-sided. A deeper and more thought-provoking question could be, "When might it be right to . . . ?" The subject of *Ethics* is related closely to *moral dilemmas,* which we cover in Chapter 7. Here are some examples of *ethical questions* teachers might pose:

- What are the ethical implications of slavery?
- Is it ever right to disobey your parents?
- When might it be ethical to kill another human being?
- What are the ethical implications of capital punishment?

The context for these questions should lie in the content of the subject matter. It becomes an exercise in *depth* when teachers relate these ethical issues to the content the students are studying in history, science, political science, or literature. Without relating the questions to the content, the responses become merely opinions based upon feelings rather than positions based upon specific criteria.

PATTERNS

Patterns are elements that repeat. There are *patterns* in sentence structure, music, history, and of course, mathematics. I prefer to have students identify both *internal* and *external patterns* in their studies. *External patterns* are those that repeat in the format and structure of textbooks. For example, how are textbooks, reference books, novels, and other books arranged? In other words, how is Chapter 1 like Chapter 2 in format? There also are *internal patterns* which occur within the context of the content. For example, students can identify the *patterns* of revolution by examining the American, French, and Bolshevik conflicts. Another example would be to identify patterns in long division problems and then compare those to the patterns in family relationships. *Now that one is a real stretch of the old dendrites!* That's all the more reason to ask such a complex question. *Patterns* are the only icon that also is listed as an *interdisciplinary theme.* (Refer to Chapter 4 for a refresher on *Interdisciplinary Themes*).

TRENDS

In my work with teachers, it has been my experience that the icon of *trends* has caused the most concern, simply because *trends* are quite difficult to see if one

(Continued)

(Continued)

hasn't been on the planet very long. However, I've been using it lately as a way for students to predict what is likely to happen next. An example of this would be asking students, "What is likely to happen next in the story and what *trends* lead you to that conclusion?" Another example would be posing a question such as, "If we examine the current state of the national economy, what *trends* do you see that might cause you to predict the President's solution to this problem?" Middle school students, in my experience, are able to see *trends* more easily when relating them to music, fashion, and movies.

DETAILS

Details, in my interpretation, are *direct quotes* from the content. When students see this icon, they know immediately that their response is going to be a direct quote. When the teacher asks students to provide a *detail* from the content, students might respond something like this: "On page 49, line 15, the author says, and I quote...." Looking for *details* helps our students become more disciplined readers. Proficient readers often *overread.* That is, they read so well, and with such speed, that they often miss crucial information. When teachers ask about *details* in this manner, however, the process becomes the precursor to research and study skills.

RULES

Rules are the parameters that establish the boundaries of our lives. In my seminars, I describe three kinds of rules as they relate to the icons:

Rules of Nature

Rules of nature are the *natural laws* that govern the universe, such as gravity, centrifugal force, survival of the fittest, and so forth. These *rules* have their roots in science and mathematics. For example, the solar system is governed by gravity, which is a rule of nature.

Rules of Law

Breaking these *rules* will get one into trouble with the law. This icon is related to legal issues, such as codes, regulations, violations, and so forth. Stealing is breaking a *rule of law,* so is jay-walking, not attending school, and so forth.

Rules of Culture

The *rules of culture* are more about *pragmatics, customs, and traditions* than about the law. If you break these *rules,* you might be viewed as impolite but probably aren't destined for jail time. Raising your hand in school is an example of a *rule of culture.* Taking off one's shoes when entering a home is another *rule of culture* in some societies.

When we ask students to describe the *kind of rule* that applies in a given context, we are asking them to examine the content in even greater *depth.* For example, students study the rules of English grammar. Teachers might ask, "Are the rules of grammar rules of *nature, law,* or *culture?* Who determines these rules? What happens if you break them?" Another question teachers might pose is just how a given rule might apply to all three kinds of rules. Grammar might relate to a *rule of nature* in that it is in the basic nature of human beings to communicate. Grammar also might be considered a *rule of law* if using it improperly in a court of law causes the judge to fine the lawyers for improper conduct. Lawyers need to choose their words well and use them wisely. Finally, grammar rules can be viewed within the context of *rules of culture* in that, as culture changes, so do rules of grammar.

BIG IDEA

Whenever my students see the icon for *big idea,* they know that they will be required to provide a *one-word summary* of the content in question, followed by a short explanation as to *why. The big idea* is one of my favorite icons because it represents my philosophy when working with bright students: *less is more!* Most bright youngsters have no trouble writing a summary; however, writing a concise summary is very difficult for them. You try it. In just one word, summarize *the big idea* of Margaret Mitchell's novel, *Gone With the Wind.* Now, explain *why* you chose the word you did. If you said the *big idea* of *Gone With the Wind* was the Civil War, sorry, you missed the point. The Civil War is the setting. The *big idea* always is an *idea,* so a correct response could be *change, courage,* or *greed.* Now, see if you can come up with a thoughtful *big idea* for the following: *The Three Little Pigs,* electricity, the Renaissance, *Pride and Prejudice,* the quadratic equation, and *The Tale of Despereaux.* Isn't this fun? We could make this a parlor game called, *What's the Big Idea?*

By the way, *big idea* is closely related to the concept of *theme* in a novel, an *era* in history, and a *concept* in science and math.

UNANSWERED QUESTIONS

The icon of *unanswered questions* is not about comprehension questions, despite the fact that a student once said, "It's an unanswered question because I haven't answered yet. When I do, it will become an answered question." That's not what

(Continued)

(Continued)

we're talking about here. Certain questions are paradoxes, conundrums, or simply questions that have confronted people for centuries. Some of these *unanswered questions* fall into the world of philosophy, such as "*If the Big Bang created the universe, what did it all look like a few seconds before the Big Bang? Is there life after death? How was it possible for the bow and arrow to be invented simultaneously on four continents at about the same time by people who had no contact with people living on other continents? Is there order to the universe? Is math invented or discovered?*" All of these questions are not only intriguing for bright students to ponder, but they allow them to confront one of the great understandings of life: *The more you know, the more you know how little you really know.* An *unanswered question* in a novel might be disclosed by the end of the novel but, for the time being, it's unanswered. An example from the *Harry Potter* series would be, "*Is Professor Snape a good guy or a bad guy?*" This question had readers pondering the answer for seven books. Eventually, the question was answered, but not before readers waded through several thousand pages.

THE ICONS OF COMPLEXITY

There are three *Icons of Complexity: multiple perspectives, change over time,* and *interdisciplinary connections.* In what follows, I describe ways to use them with students.

MULTIPLE PERSPECTIVES

This icon of *multiple perspectives* requires students to see a situation, event, character, or concept from a *different point of view.* For example, a teacher might ask students to take a *different perspective* than the author of a specific article from a newspaper or magazine. First, students must identify the *point of view* of the writer. This actually is the hardest part, especially when looking at a textbook. Students often are surprised to learn that their textbooks are written from a specific *point of view* or *slant.* Situations in which the characters in stories *find* themselves also can be viewed from *different perspectives.* I like the concept of *multiple perspectives* rather than *different perspectives,* because often there are more than two ways to view something. Looking at an event or issue from an unpopular position might mean that students actually have to take a position other than one they personally support. Sounds like the high school debate team, doesn't it? In practice, student teams are assigned opposing views on an issue, *euthanasia,* for example, and must share multiple arguments with the class that support a variety of positions. This activity certainly encourages students to listen to one other. When we can see another's *point of view,* we see the content or issue *more complexly.*

CHANGE OVER TIME

Examining how a topic, concept, or content piece has *changed over time* or *evolved* is another example of *complex thinking*. Asking how something has changed over time, such as a character in a novel, religion, or the role of women, requires students to examine the content in the past and present, and it possibly requires them to predict the future. Earlier we examined rules related to the content of English grammar. Asking students to trace the evolution and changes in grammar and spelling over time introduces a whole new level of complexity to this subject. Students can examine how they personally have *changed over time* and then predict what they might be doing in 20 years, based upon the *patterns* and *rules* that they live by today. When students read a current event from a newspaper, they might respond to the question of how the issue has changed over time and what further changes might take place in the future.

INTERDISCIPLINARY CONNECTIONS

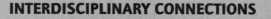

"How is what we studied this morning about electricity related to the Age of Exploration and the voyage of Magellan?" What a great thought-provoking question! Of course, *you* don't have to answer the question. After all, you're the teacher and your job is to *ask* the hard questions. How are the content pieces of our curriculum *interrelated?* Our brain is a pattern-seeking organ that makes connections between concepts, content, facts, and ideas. Asking students to make these connections encourages *complex thinking*.

Some textbooks outline these connections *for* students. What a shame! Asking students to make these connections themselves not only increases meaning for them, but it also creates patterns to help them see how things are connected.

Sometimes, connections are found *within the discipline:*

- In the Scott O'Dell novels, in what ways are the characters of Zia and Karana similar?
- How is *Tales of a Fourth Grade Nothing* similar to *The Lion, the Witch and the Wardrobe?*

Sometimes connections are *between two disciplines:*

- Describe the connection between the invention of the camera and the rise of impressionism in the art world.
- How are the procedures for solving this math problem similar to those for solving a problem in economics, or science, or in your social life?

When teachers regularly ask students to explain how one area of study relates to other subjects, rather than telling them, *the students are the ones getting smarter!*

TEACHING THE ICONS OF DEPTH AND COMPLEXITY

Like any new concept, the *Icons of Depth and Complexity* first must be *taught* to students. I wouldn't try to teach more than one or two of the icons per day. In fact, my suggestion for teachers is, *an icon a day keeps confusion away!* Here is an example of how a teacher might begin:

> Today we will be examining the concept of *multiple perspectives,* one of the *Icons of Complexity.* The picture for this idea is a pair of glasses. Why is this picture a good representation of *multiple perspectives?* In our lesson today we will be reading the story of *Katie's Trunk* from our anthology. As we read the story, look at the events from the perspective of each character: Katie, her parents, the rebels who break into their home, and the Tories who support the King of England. See how many different points of view you can find and we'll write them on the chart when we finish the story.

MISUSING THE ICONS

The *Icons of Depth and Complexity* can be great visual aids to help focus teachers and students on deeper and more complex thinking. However, displaying the icons around the room or creating bulletin boards won't help students unless teachers intentionally use them on a daily basis. Having the icons placed around the classroom, but never using them, makes them just decoration, like wallpaper. Don't worry about finding the perfect lesson or the best time to use the icons. Just start using them so that they become an integral part of every lesson and every discussion.

FLEXIBILITY IN USING THE ICONS

One of the pitfalls for teachers is trying to incorporate all of the *Icons of Depth and Complexity.* My suggestion is to begin using the icons that make the most sense to you and then branching out to incorporate others. Teachers have the flexibility to pick and choose which icons to use, based upon your own understanding of them and the level of the students with whom you work. Remember: the goal of using the *Icons of Depth and Complexity* is to have students apply them to content in order to gain deeper meaning. The following strategy was shared with me by Dawn Romo, a fifth-grade teacher, who focuses on one icon each day.

ICON OF THE DAY

The teacher selects one icon each day, posts it in front of the class, and references it in every lesson that day. For example, if the icon is *rules,* then at the beginning of instruction, the teacher tells students to watch for any kind of *rules* in the lesson. Then, at the end of every lesson, the teacher asks students to share which *rules* they found and to determine if they are *rules of nature, rules of law,* or *rules of culture.* Students will find *rules* in mathematics, reading, science, grammar, and even recess!

USING FRAMES AS AN EDUCATIONAL TOOL

Visualize a picture frame. Better yet, look at the ones I have drawn for you here. In the center of the frame is where a picture normally is placed, while the side panels provide decoration to enhance the picture. When these frames are used as an educational tool, they have far more to do with enhancing and extending understanding (*depth* and *complexity*) than merely providing decoration.

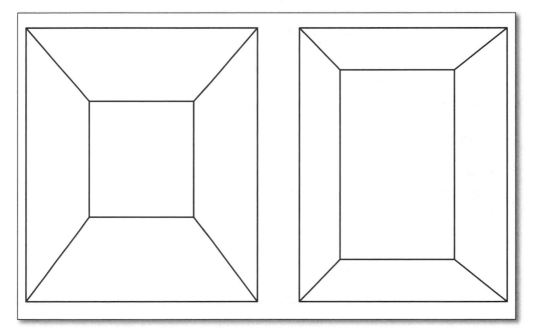

USING FRAMES WITH THE ICONS OF DEPTH AND COMPLEXITY

Educational frames can be used in a variety of ways as instructional tools: charts, visual aids, graphic organizers, study guides, and so forth.

However, we focus on a few strategies for using frames specifically with the *Icons of Depth and Complexity.*

Frames are such a visual educational tool, that the best way I can explain how to use them is to show you, so I've created an example here. The example provided is used with the story, *Katie's Trunk,* from the fifth-grade anthology written by Ann Turner. It will be most helpful if you read my explanation while looking at the visual that follows. When the two pages are used together, it should be easier to make sense of the example.

AN EXAMPLE FOR USING A FRAME
WITH THE STORY *KATIE'S TRUNK*

- The center of the frame
  - At the top, students write the title of the content they will be examining for depth and complexity: *Katie's Trunk.*
  - Under the title, students write the three major events in the story, which provide their summary.
- The side panels of the frame
  - Four icons are selected, one for each of the four panels of the frame.
  - A related question is written next to each icon.
  - Students write an answer to each question in the appropriate panel of the frame.

OTHER SUGGESTIONS FOR USING FRAMES

When first using frames with students, the teacher might assign specific icons for each section of the frame and provide the appropriate questions. As students become more adept at using the frames, and more flexible and complex in their thinking processes, they can select the icons and related questions themselves. Remember the value of *underexplaining: The less information teachers provide, the more students have to work, and the smarter they become!*

You can adjust the size of the frames, depending upon the assignment. If you want students to write a paragraph summary, as in the example on the next page, you can make the center of the frame larger. Just adapt the frame to work for you. One teacher had students write the *big idea* in the center and illustrate it with a symbol, which is much more sophisticated than drawing a picture of their favorite part. In the example for *Katie's Trunk,* a one-word summary might be *rebelliousness,* or it could be *perception.* Having students draw a picture representing these two *big ideas* is even more complex. If you are interested in more ideas for using frames,

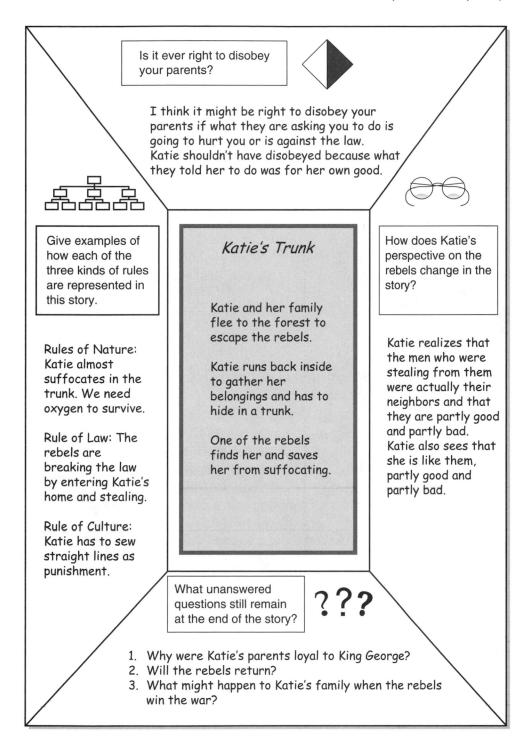

Is it ever right to disobey your parents?

I think it might be right to disobey your parents if what they are asking you to do is going to hurt you or is against the law. Katie shouldn't have disobeyed because what they told her to do was for her own good.

Give examples of how each of the three kinds of rules are represented in this story.

Katie's Trunk

Katie and her family flee to the forest to escape the rebels.

Katie runs back inside to gather her belongings and has to hide in a trunk.

One of the rebels finds her and saves her from suffocating.

How does Katie's perspective on the rebels change in the story?

Rules of Nature: Katie almost suffocates in the trunk. We need oxygen to survive.

Rule of Law: The rebels are breaking the law by entering Katie's home and stealing.

Rule of Culture: Katie has to sew straight lines as punishment.

Katie realizes that the men who were stealing from them were actually their neighbors and that they are partly good and partly bad. Katie also sees that she is like them, partly good and partly bad.

What unanswered questions still remain at the end of the story?

???

1. Why were Katie's parents loyal to King George?
2. Will the rebels return?
3. What might happen to Katie's family when the rebels win the war?

I recommend the book by Sandra Kaplan and Bette Gould, *Frames: Differentiating the Core Curriculum* (1999).

STRATEGIES FOR USING THE ICONS OF DEPTH AND COMPLEXITY

We have addressed ways teachers might introduce the icons to students and how to use the icons in educational frames. Now let's look at some more strategies for using the *Icons of Depth and Complexity*. Paula Wilkes and Mark Szymanski, in their new book, *The Deep and Complex Look Book* (2009), present a great idea for doing a research report. Each of the icons becomes a page in a research report so that by the time students have completed their reports, they have taken a *deep* and *complex* look at the topic. Beats the heck out of a diorama made with plastic dinosaurs! This book has lots of other great ideas for addressing *depth* and *complexity*. Read on for more ideas.

DIVIDE AND CONQUER

This is a popular strategy I use in my seminars to show teachers how to use the *Icons of Depth and Complexity*. The entire class reads the same literary selection, but each table group has a different icon card. Using its assigned icon, each table group reflects on the content and share back with the rest of the class, either verbally or using a visual. For example, the group with *details* might select an important quote, write it on the board, and explain why it was chosen. The *big idea* group could explain why the one word it selected summarizes the content. There are 11 icons, so some might be used twice and others not at all, depending upon the number of table groups. Recording each group's contribution on a chart provides an even deeper and more complex look at the content when all icon responses are included.

BOOK REPORTS

When our son was in elementary school, he selected *Charlotte's Web* for his book report and did a diorama, a common assignment. Although he received an A on the book report, he never read the book. How does a student get an A on a book report without reading the book? Easy, use the illustrations to create a fabulous diorama. Our son's diorama was spectacular! (He's very artistic.) Isn't there something wrong with an assignment that allows a student to get an A without doing the real work intended, namely reading the book? Asking students to tell you their favorite part of the book or why they liked it isn't particularly deep either; neither is having them draw a picture. Teachers might consider incorporating the *Icons of Depth and Complexity* as part of their book report format. As you have seen from the *Katie's Trunk* example, frames work well for book reports. In addition, you might have students put the following sentence frame on the backs of their book report and use it to provide a summary:

Book: _____

(Someone) _____ wanted _____

but _____

so _____.

Let's take another look at this sentence frame and apply it to *Charlotte's Web:*

Book: *Charlotte's Web* by E. B. White

Templeton the Rat **wanted** first crack at all the food in the barnyard trough, **but** he was the lowest animal in the barnyard hierarchy and was only allowed to have scraps that the other animals didn't want. **So** he agreed to help Charlotte find words on pieces of newspaper to weave into her web on the condition that he would be allowed to eat first out of the trough.

Couple this sentence frame with any four of the *Icons of Depth and Complexity,* and now we have a more rigorous book report. There is no way my son could have completed this type of report without reading the book. By the way, our son is grown up now and, since he's a veterinarian, I bought him *Charlotte's Web.* I thought it was about time he actually read it!

CURRENT EVENTS

I've noticed over the last few years that teachers are using newspapers and magazines in classrooms less and less. I understand that the Internet has provided us with news articles online. However, teachers never seem to have time to incorporate current events into the curriculum. Every week or so we hear of a newspaper that is ceasing publication. It appears that the public is relying on television news celebrities and radio talk show hosts to provide information and most citizens simply take them at their word. This trend concerns me because all students, not just our brightest youngsters, need to hear *multiple perspectives* about what is going on locally, on a national scale, and internationally, not just about what celebrity is getting divorced this week. For these reasons, I'm an advocate for discussing current events in the classroom. However, let's look at ways we can make current events more relevant by using the *Icons of Depth and Complexity.*

A NEW TWIST ON CURRENT EVENTS

1. Teachers can bring in a single newspaper. (No need for 30 copies of *The New York Times.*) Place the newspaper on a table in the back of the room and, when they have time, have students cut out one article each that seems interesting to them. (*USA Today* is a great newspaper for elementary school kids because it's written at a fifth-grade level. Save *The Wall Street Journal* for the high school classes.)

2. Pair up students, telling them to keep their current event a secret from their partner.

3. Students each are to read the first two or three paragraphs of the current event and highlight all the *language of the discipline* words (the technical vocabulary), including acronyms, jargon, and words that are related to the content. For example, an article about a robbery probably would have words related to law enforcement and criminology.

Depending upon the time available, the teacher might have students add one or more of the following strategies for increasing *depth* and *complexity.* Over time, you might try all of them, but probably not all at once.

GUESS MY TOPIC

Students take turns reading their *language of the discipline* words to their partner who attempts to guess what the article is about after each word clue is given. Each word clue, and subsequent guess, helps narrow the guesses until the topic finally is identified. This activity involves *deductive* reasoning. You've just created a game: *Guess My Topic!*

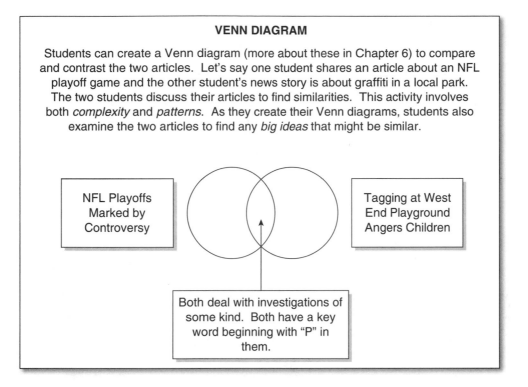

VENN DIAGRAM

Students can create a Venn diagram (more about these in Chapter 6) to compare and contrast the two articles. Let's say one student shares an article about an NFL playoff game and the other student's news story is about graffiti in a local park. The two students discuss their articles to find similarities. This activity involves both *complexity* and *patterns*. As they create their Venn diagrams, students also examine the two articles to find any *big ideas* that might be similar.

NFL Playoffs Marked by Controversy

Tagging at West End Playground Angers Children

Both deal with investigations of some kind. Both have a key word beginning with "P" in them.

SENTENCE FRAMES

Students might complete a *sentence frame* about the article, like the one used for book reports, or they can create their own.

SUMMARIES

Students could write summaries of their articles. Here is a strategy I learned from Diane Snyder, a fourth-grade teacher, who used *Weekly Readers* for current events. She had students use the *language of the discipline* words as a guide for summarizing their articles. Students were instructed to include all the *language of the discipline* words in their summary, in the order in which they appeared in the article. What a great idea! The resulting summaries were far better than before.

OTHER ICONS TO CONSIDER

Recently, additional icons have been created by teachers for specific subjects or disciplines. Melanie Montgomery has developed a set of icons specific to mathematics, *Math Icon Cards* (2006). A teacher in one of my classes shared a set of icons he developed for use with his secondary history classes. They were used as a way of outlining each chapter of the textbook. Over the years, other educators have substituted different icons for the originals. Here are the ones that I've used:

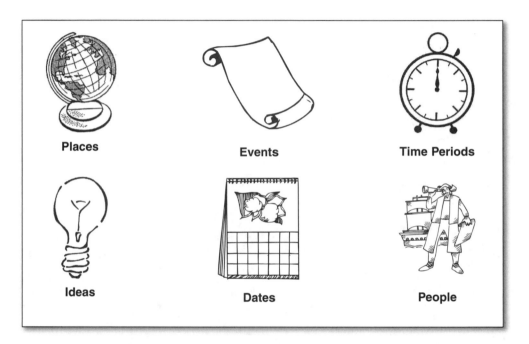

SOME FINAL THOUGHTS

This chapter describes a variety of strategies which use the *Icons of Depth and Complexity.* Experiment with them and incorporate your own ideas. Some teachers have altered some of these symbols to make them easier to draw. (Example: using a pair of glasses as the picture to symbolize *multiple perspectives.*) There always are new ideas being devised by teachers all over the country. Try Googling the *Icons of Depth and Complexity* and see what you can find. Remember, the intent of using the icons is to encourage students to think in deep and complex ways. The icons are but one instructional tool to achieve this goal. In the next chapter, we explore *questioning strategies*, another tool for teachers to differentiate instruction.

6 Questioning Strategies

INTRODUCTION

Questioning strategies are one of the most important instructional skills for teachers to use. Once mastered, these strategies can be applied to any content and used with students of all abilities. There are many models for questioning that have been developed. The one I use most in my seminars is the structure provided in the 1950s and 1960s by Benjamin Bloom because most teachers are familiar with it. This chapter describes how to use Bloom's Taxonomy with students by relating it to the four components of differentiation: *depth, complexity, novelty,* and *acceleration/pacing.* I focus on the *analysis* level of the taxonomy and the three types of *analytical thinking: classification analysis, structure analysis,* and *operation analysis.*

INDUCTIVE AND DEDUCTIVE REASONING

Questions can be divided into two general classifications: those requiring *deductive* reasoning and those requiring *inductive* reasoning. Both aspects of thinking are equally valuable and teachers should be aware that both types of questions are necessary for students to develop critical thinking skills.

Deductive reasoning is the method used to find *the correct answer* by deducing from the data given. This type of reasoning is used by detectives to determine who committed the crime. Literary figures, such as Hercule Poirot, Miss Marple, Sherlock Holmes, and Sam Spade, used *deductive reasoning.*

Television characters like Jessica Fletcher, Adrian Monk, and the CSI investigators use *deductive reasoning.* Most problem-solving activities in school are *deductive.* Students look at evidence and then try to find the answer to the question. This type of reasoning is closely associated with *depth* and *complexity.*

Inductive reasoning requires creative problem solving. This type of reasoning seeks to find *multiple solutions* to a problem. In the classroom, inductive activities include brainstorming and open-ended tasks. This type of reasoning is closely associated with *complexity* and *novelty.* Doctors on television medical programs, such as *House, Miami Medical,* and *ER,* often use *inductive reasoning.* They look at their patient's symptoms and think of all the possible diagnoses before narrowing down the possibilities.

In the classroom, solving a math problem is *deductive,* while coming up with alternate ways to solve the problem is *inductive.* Playing *20 Questions* and *Animal, Vegetable, or Mineral* are *deductive reasoning* activities. Brainstorming everything you can think of that is associated with salamanders is *inductive.*

As we examine questioning strategies, note how both deductive and inductive reasoning relate to Bloom's Taxonomy.

USING BLOOM'S TAXONOMY

In 1956, Benjamin Bloom and a team of psychologists developed a classification of levels of intellectual behavior which led to a hierarchy of questioning, from simple to complex. In the 1990s, Bloom and others rearranged the hierarchy and updated it to reflect more recent research. In education circles, *knowledge* (remembering) and *comprehension* (understanding) are considered lower level questions, while *application* (applying), analysis (analyzing), synthesis (creating), and evaluation (evaluating) are considered higher level questions. Until recently, the majority of classroom time has been devoted to addressing knowledge and comprehension questions, while most real-life situations require us to use higher level questions of application, analysis, synthesis, and evaluation. In response to this dilemma, current standardized tests have made a significant shift in the types of questions asked to focus on the higher levels of thinking. As a result of this new focus on standardized tests and the kinds of questions they use, classroom instruction has changed to emphasize higher level thinking skills. Let's take a closer look at the hierarchy of questioning from the original version of *Bloom's Taxonomy* and apply it to questioning strategies.

KNOWLEDGE LEVEL QUESTIONS

Questions at the *knowledge level* are looking for one correct answer and can be found easily in the text or content source. Although not necessarily easy, these questions don't require interpretation or deep understanding; they frequently require only a rote response. Examples of questions at the *knowledge level* include factual information and basic arithmetic computation. However, teachers certainly can differentiate *knowledge level* questions for their students and are encouraged to do so. The game Trivial Pursuit is all about *knowledge level* questions. Just watch *Jeopardy* on television to see that knowledge level questions can be difficult. *Knowledge level questions* can be compared to the *language of the discipline,* an icon of *depth* discussed in the previous chapter. Knowing vocabulary and technical terms are all important knowledge activities. When teachers focus on more rigorous and complex vocabulary, they are addressing the differentiation component of *depth.*

COMPREHENSION LEVEL QUESTIONS

Comprehension questions seek out answers that require a greater degree of understanding of the content. The answer usually is more than a one-word response and might require students to explain a concept or term. There is a *correct answer* to comprehension questions. Explaining how something works, describing the plot of a story or novel, summarizing, and solving math problems are examples of *comprehension level* questions. Again, the degree of difficulty determines the academic rigor. A student, who responds that the cause of the Civil War is slavery, is not nearly as comprehensive a thinker as one who can provide multiple causes of the war and important events and influences. Comprehension questions require more in-depth thinking than knowledge level questions. Now, let's move into the higher level thinking skills.

APPLICATION LEVEL QUESTIONS

Questions at the *application level* ask students to do something with the content. They may be asked to relate what they have learned to another topic or to explain the relevance of what they learned to another situation. This level of questioning, and the levels which follow, are considered higher order thinking skills. If teachers ask students to relate the content to their year-long theme, it is an *application level* question. When students discuss issues of relevancy, such as "Why is it important to know algebra," they are addressing *application level* questions. Taking content and using it to produce a product or project is an *application level* skill. Application is associated *complexity*. The three brain output activities of *talking, writing,* and *creating* are closely associated with the *application level* of thinking.

ANALYSIS LEVEL QUESTIONS

Analysis level questions ask students to take apart what they are learning in one of three ways:

- **Classification Analysis**—Asks students to take apart content according to attributes or characteristics. These questions ask students to determine the *kinds* of elements in a content piece.
- **Structure Analysis**—Asks students to take apart the content according to its *parts.* Sometimes the parts are physical, like the *parts* of a flower. Other times they are elemental, like the *parts* of a novel.
- **Operation Analysis**—Asks students to take apart the content according to the *order* or sequence in which it occurred.

Analytical thinking is *complex* thinking. Later in this chapter, we look more closely at the three aspects of analysis, along with activities and strategies that relate to each.

SYNTHESIS LEVEL QUESTIONS

Questions at the *synthesis level* put content together in new ways. This level is the creative component of critical thinking. A new ending for a story, a scenario asking "what if," projects, and open-ended assignments fall under this category. Asking students to explain a new way to solve a math problem is another example. When we ask students the *big idea* of involving content, we are asking a *synthesis* question. The completion of a project is a *synthesis activity* because many elements must be put together to create the finished product. Synthesis assignments usually are open-ended tasks which require students to generate some original thoughts about a question or topic with more than one possible answer. Synthesis is closely associated with both *complexity* and *novelty.*

EVALUATION LEVEL QUESTIONS

For many years, Benjamin Bloom believed that *evaluation* was the highest form of thinking. Later in his career, through additional research, he determined that *synthesis* is more complex and is the highest level. In either case, *evaluation* is one of the most important skills of thinking and one that is closely related to living in the real world. *Evaluation level* questions ask students to use criteria to judge ethical issues associated with the content. This view of evaluation is far more rigorous than asking the student, "Did you like the book?" *Evaluation* questions might have students judge the actions of characters in a story or historical event in light of moral issues, implications, influences, and context. A major component of *evaluation* for students is self-evaluation of their work, their thinking, and their conduct. Lessons using moral dilemmas, Socratic questioning, and open-ended tasks are all part of *evaluation.* These types of questions are closely associated with *complexity* and *novelty* in differentiation.

CORRELATIONS BETWEEN INSTRUCTIONAL STRATEGIES

To help teachers see the correlations and interrelatedness of instructional strategies, I created the following chart to show how the elements of *Bloom's Taxonomy,* the *Four Components of Differentiation,* and the *Icons of Depth and Complexity* are related.

Bloom's Taxonomy	Components of Differentiation	Icons of Depth and Complexity
Knowledge	Depth	Language of the Discipline
Comprehension	Depth	Details
Application	Complexity	Trends & Patterns
Analysis	Complexity & Depth	Rules, Change Over Time, & Interdisciplinary Relationships
Synthesis	Complexity & Novelty	Big Idea
Evaluation	Complexity & Depth	Ethics, Multiple Perspectives, Unanswered Questions

THE THREE TYPES OF ANALYTICAL THINKING

We look more closely at *analytical thinking* through assignments and activities teachers can use with students.

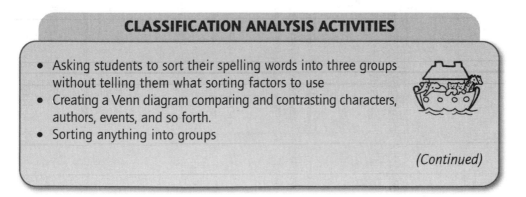

CLASSIFICATION ANALYSIS ACTIVITIES

- Asking students to sort their spelling words into three groups without telling them what sorting factors to use
- Creating a Venn diagram comparing and contrasting characters, authors, events, and so forth.
- Sorting anything into groups

(Continued)

(Continued)

- Asking students to describe the attributes of something
- Completing a *concept development lesson* (described later in this chapter)
- Completing a *word link* diagram (described later in this chapter)

Asking students to sort any content and telling them how to sort the content, that is, sorting spelling words into groups according to the parts of speech, is a *comprehension* activity. However, when we *underexplain* the assignment by asking students to sort their spelling words without giving them any further explanation, then we have moved up to the *analysis level*. The more we specify what we want students to do, the less they have to think on their own. Having students create a Venn diagram about three novels, three historical events, and so forth, is more beneficial than simply asking them to write a report which they might just copy or paraphrase from a reference book or the Internet.

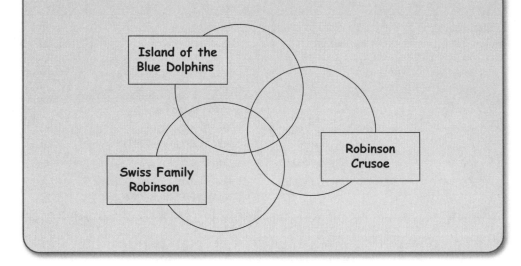

STRUCTURAL ANALYSIS ACTIVITIES

- Asking students to diagram a sentence
- Using graphic organizers
- Labeling the parts of something
- Drawing a diagram of something
- Creating a poster
- Building a model
- Taking something apart and labeling the parts
- Creating a web to describe a concept

There are a number of activities for students that involve *structural analysis.* Here are some suggestions:

- Building the circulatory system out of Legos
- Taking apart a flower and labeling its parts (far superior to a worksheet)
- Reconstructing the bones of a digested rodent from owl pellets
- Taking apart broken electrical appliances (be sure to cut off electrical cords first!) and then drawing and labeling each part
- Drawing blueprints and scale drawings of familiar items or of their homes
- Building model airplanes, boats, cars, and so forth, from kits
- Assembling jigsaw puzzles
- Playing games such as Scrabble, Boggle, and Sudoku

OPERATION ANALYSIS ACTIVITIES

- Writing the steps or procedures for solving a math problem
- Outlining a chapter from the textbook
- Designing a flowchart to explain a procedure
- Creating a timeline
- Putting something in order (chronological, hierarchical, etc.)

Anytime we ask students to put something in order, we are asking them to perform an *operation analysis.* Timelines are an excellent way to conceptualize history. Higher ability and older students can construct a two-tiered timeline.

For example, students create a timeline. Historical events, taken from content being studied, such as the explorers, can be placed above the line. (Henry Hudson explored eastern Canada; Vasco de Gama explored the Mississippi, etc.) Below the line, students could find other events in history that occurred around the same time.

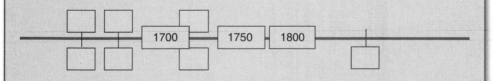

The events above the line correlate to the specific content of the curriculum. Events below the line might relate to a specific topic such as technology, music, art, science, everyday life, and so forth. Students might research the events on the bottom, draw a picture to represent them, or write a short explanation for the timeline. This kind of complex activity broadens thinking and allows

(Continued)

(Continued)

students to see that not everything in the world happened in America. There are many source books for teachers and students to use for their timeline research which help provide a more global view of world events. One of my favorites is *The Timetables of History* by Bernard Grun (2005).

Another activity for students using *operation analysis* is to have them write out the steps to the solution of a math problem. Tell them not to do the problem, just explain *how* to do the problem. Whenever we ask students to describe the steps or procedures for doing something, we are asking them to use *operation analysis*.

AN ACTIVITY TO TEST YOUR MEMORY

On the following page is a series of objects. Set the timer and study the pictures for *30 seconds*. Then close the book and write down as many of the items as you can remember. Once you have finished, open the book and check to see how well you did.

STRATEGIES FOR MEMORIZING

Now, don't worry about how many you got right in the previous exercise. It isn't about that. It's about what strategies you used for memorizing the objects. After reading the following section, you might repeat the exercise to see if you can remember a few more items.

Think about how you recalled the objects on the previous page. What strategies did you use? Did you use any of those listed in the following box?

MEMORIZATION STRATEGIES

- Group items according to categories (food items, clothing items, etc.).
- Remember their physical location on the page (visualizing the page).
- Make up a quick story which uses each object (following a sequence).
- Create a pneumonic device (remembering the first letter of each object).

Did you count the items? (By the way, there were 13.)

Let's consider *analytical thinking* and look again at the strategies you used in order to remember the objects in the previous activity. When you grouped the items into categories, you used *classification analysis*. If you remembered them because of their physical location on the page, that's *structural analysis*. Telling yourself a story to remember the items is using *operation analysis*. Creating a rhyme using the first letter of each item is using *structural analysis.* Counting the objects is called *validation*. Okay, validation isn't a form of analysis but it helped you determine whether you missed any items. For example, if I asked you to write the names of all the states, you know there are 50 of them, so if you forget any, you can work backwards. You might choose to write down the states according to alphabetical order (*classification analysis*), or from east to west (structural analysis), or starting with the states you have visited (*operational analysis*). If you remembered the states from a song you learned, then that's also *operational analysis*. The point is, there isn't a *right* way; it's whatever works for you.

Students who struggle with memorization have no strategies to use. They simply stare at the content and hope for the best. Students who group by concepts, look for structures, or use pneumonic devices fare better every time. Memorization is one of the most important aspects of knowledge acquisition and is aligned closely with *analysis* in that the strategies used to memorize often are part of *analytical thinking.*

ANOTHER MEMORIZATION ACTIVITY

Now, go ahead and list the presidents of the United States. Before you do, what strategy will you use?

TWO STRATEGIES FOR PROCESSING INFORMATION

The following strategies, *Word-Links* and *Concept Development*, are designed to give students opportunities to *process* and *organize* information. I created *Word-Links* to help students in processing vocabulary, and Taba, Durkin, Fraenkel, and NcNaughton (1971) developed *Concept Development* as a way for them to organize information.

WORD-LINKS

Word-Links is a vocabulary activity that encourages the creative use of language. It begins *deductively* and concludes *inductively*. It focuses on *knowledge* and *comprehension* at the beginning of the activity but ends with *analysis* and *synthesis*. In the lexicon of *differentiation*, the activity begins with an emphasis on *depth* and concludes with an emphasis on *complexity*. The diagram on the following page is one that teachers can provide for their students. Following the blank diagram is one that has been completed by a group of students.

The *Word-Links* activity begins with a *seed word*. It can be a word related to your content or simply one chosen at random. Once the *seed word* is selected, the teacher asks students to provide a sentence using that word. This is the part of the activity that addresses *depth*. If you refer to the completed diagram while reading the example in the box, this activity will be easier to understand.

WORD-LINKS EXAMPLE
TO BE USED WITH THE DIAGRAM ON PAGE 81

The seed word is *GATE*. A student says, "Sammy is in the *GATE* class." The teacher then asks the class to provide a *synonym* for the word *GATE* as it was used in the

(Continued)

(Continued)

sentence. The students determine that *GATE* in this sentence means *gifted.* The teacher writes that in one of the boxes underneath the word GATE on the diagram.

Next, the teacher asks if students can provide another sentence using the word GATE in a different way. Students suggest, "The girl opened the *gate* to the garden." And they provide the word *entrance* as a synonym, which the teacher writes in the other box underneath the seed word. This process continues. As long as the spelling is accurate, the word can be used in any way the students wish. *GATE* can be an acronym for *Gifted and Talented Education,* and it also can mean a *garden gate.* On the second level, the word *entrance* can mean *appearance,* as in the sentence, "The actress made a grand *entrance* into the room." But *entrance* can also mean to *enchant.* It's spelled the same but pronounced differently: "The wicked witch sought to *entrance* the children into believing she was their friend." *Entrance* in this sense can mean *hypnotize.*

The teacher continues down the diagram following the lines, always asking the students to use the word in a sentence. If students cannot think of an alternate meaning to a given word, the teacher can provide a sentence that might help them see a new meaning. If the teacher cannot think of one, then students are asked to use the word in another sentence and use a synonym of the word with the same meaning.

Once the class has arrived at the middle of the diagram, the thinking skills shift from *knowledge* and *comprehension* to *analysis* and *synthesis.* This is the *complexity* part of the activity. The students now are asked to put two words together, following the lines of the diagram, to form a link between the two and then to come up with a word that connects them together. For example, the two words are *hypnotize* and *show.* Students decided that *hypnosis* in a *show* is designed to *entertain.* This process continues until a final word is selected to join the last two words at the bottom of the diagram. The last part of the activity is to create a link between the final word and the first word on the diagram. Students then write a short explanation as to how they determined the final link. Refer to the sample I have provided.

ADAPTING AND GRADING WORD-LINKS

The example provided explains *Word-Links* as a class activity; however, it can be used in the same way with smaller groups and also with individual students. Teachers frequently ask how to grade such an activity. If a grade must be assigned, my suggestion is to look at the *seed word* (provided by the teacher) and the *final word* (determined by the student), and then grade the student's explanation as to how the two words are connected. In the sample provided, the *seed word* is GATE, and the *final word* is *agent.* The link given is *guard* because *a guard is an agent who secures a gate.*

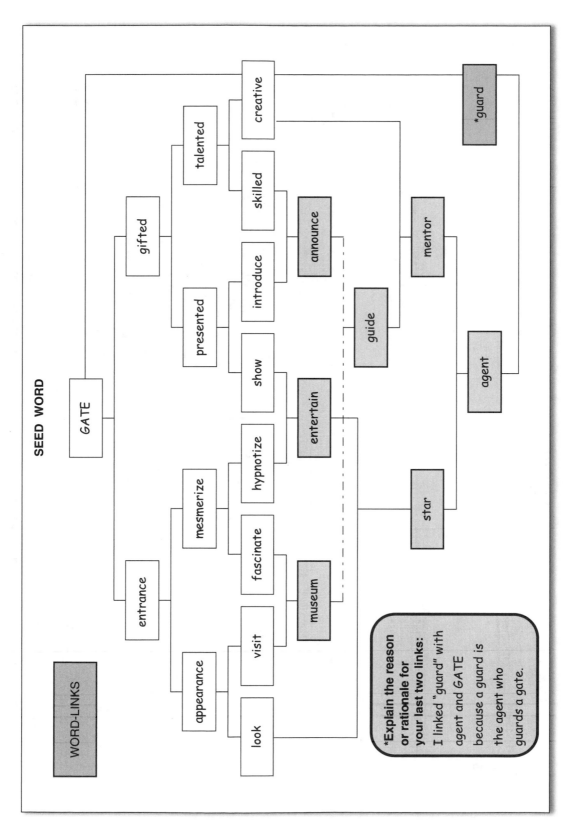

WORD-LINKS

SEED WORD

GATE

*Explain the reason or rationale for your last two links:
I linked "guard" with agent and GATE because a guard is the agent who guards a gate.

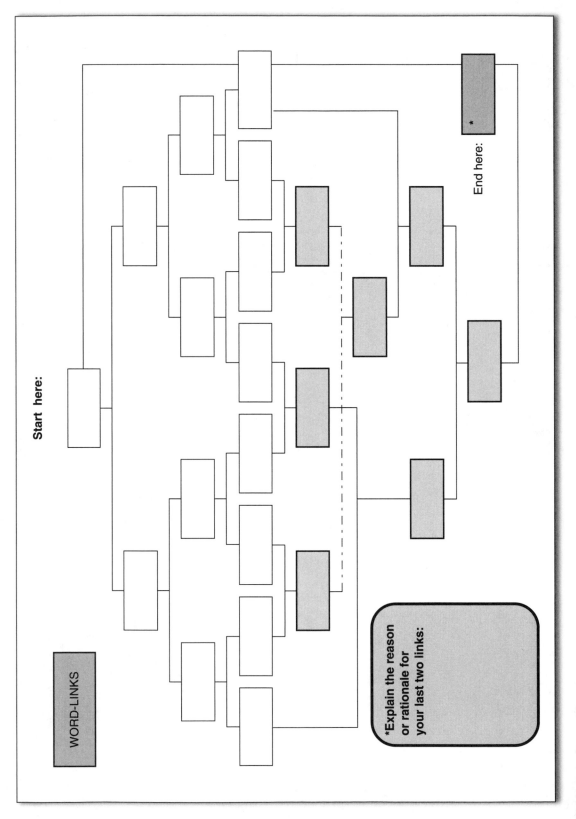

Start here:

End here:

WORD-LINKS

*Explain the reason or rationale for your last two links:

WORD-LINKS FOR PRIMARY GRADES

Over the years, I have shared *Word-Links* with hundreds of teachers in my seminars. Many primary teachers would like to use this strategy but find the diagram a bit daunting for younger students. Therefore, I created a modified diagram, as shown here, that works well for younger students:

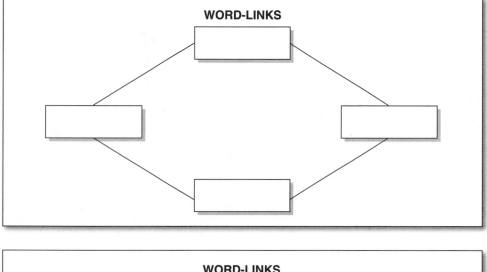

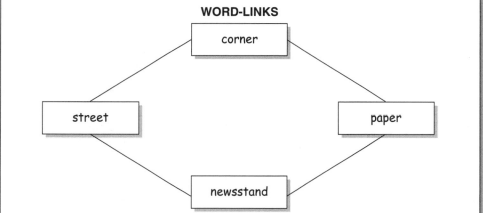

Here is a completed diagram using *corner* as the seed word. In this example, students show that *corner* is associated with *street*, as well as with *paper*, since both have *corners*. Putting these words together conceptually, they might think of a *newsstand*. Teachers can extend this simple *Word-Link* diagram further by starting with *newsstand*.

THE CONCEPT DEVELOPMENT MODEL

Another strategy that incorporates both *depth* and *complexity* is *concept development*. This lesson model, created by educator Hilda Taba in 1966, is so associated with her that it also is called Taba's Model. I've adapted Taba's Model for use in my seminars, which is how it is presented here. Because she believed that students make generalizations only after data are organized, Taba's Concept Development Model contains three parts: brainstorming, sorting, and diagramming. This model can be used effectively at the beginning of a unit of study to find out what students already know about a topic or at the end of a unit to determine what students have learned.

STEPS IN A CONCEPT DEVELOPMENT LESSON

In preparation for a lesson, students divide their paper into three columns as shown in the following diagram:

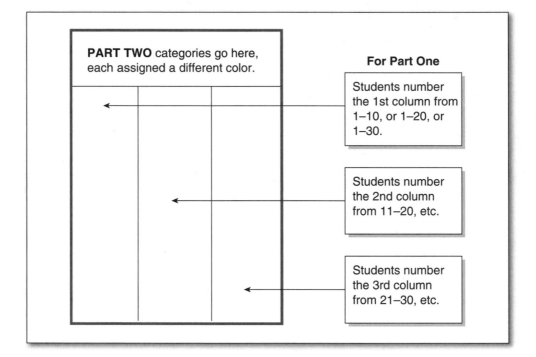

Part 1: Brainstorming—*Emphasis on depth, knowledge/comprehension, and inductive reasoning*

Step 1: Students may work as a whole class, in small groups, or individually. They use a blank sheet of paper, dividing and numbering it as shown in the example, according to the number of words to be used. (The number of words is dictated by the age of the students: about 10 words per column for primary, about 20 for sixth grade, and perhaps 30 for secondary students.) The teacher provides a topic and students compete, either individually or in groups, to think of words related to the topic and write them in the first column. (If working in groups, students should designate a recorder. This job might be passed from one person to another after each column is completed.) When a third of the class has completed the first column, the teacher calls *time* and everyone stops.

Step 2: Students are asked to come up with 10, 20, or 30 *additional* words for the second column, associated with the same topic. They may not repeat any of the words already used in the first column.

Step 3: Between the second and third columns, students are allowed to share with each other to get some additional ideas. Students then complete the third column of words, either individually or in their groups, according to how the teacher has set up the activity. Once again, when a third of the students are done, the teacher calls *time*.

Part 1 of the lesson is designed to help students recall as much information as possible about a given topic. Students work very fast and furiously; when a third of the students are done, move on. Here is an example of what a paper might look like after Part 1 is completed:

EXAMPLE: The topic is SPORTS

baseball	sailing	net
basketball	Scuba diving	badminton
swimming	hot air balloon	flag football
track	goal	cleats
marathon	goalie	boxing
skiing	inning	wrestling
diving	bases	area
ping pong	pads	judge
weightlifting	helmets	tickets
tennis	knee guards	season
football	referee	golf
lacrosse	umpire	clubs
field hockey	fans	court
ice skating	stadium	bowling
ice dancing	Yankees	curling
snowboarding	Cardinals	bobsledding
skateboarding	Eagles	shuffleboard
surfing	Dodgers	arm wrestling
bungie jumping	Rams	gymnastics
soccer	Raiders	dressage

Part 2: Sorting—*Emphasis on Complexity,*
Analysis, and Deductive Reasoning

Step 1: Students examine their completed list of 30–90 words and determine three to five broad categories.

Step 2: Students write these categories above the line at the top of the page and assign a different colored marking pen to each category. (*Miscellaneous* or *Other* can't be categories; all words must fit into a specific category. Some teachers excuse up to 5% of the words if they don't fit into one of the designated categories.)

Step 3: Students review their lists of words in the three columns and assign each word a colored dot which corresponds to the category at the top of the page. I created the colored dot method because words do not have to be rewritten under each category and it saves time.

Part 2 of the lesson involves classification analysis because students classify their words by categories. Here is an example of what the top part of the paper might look like after categories have been determined.

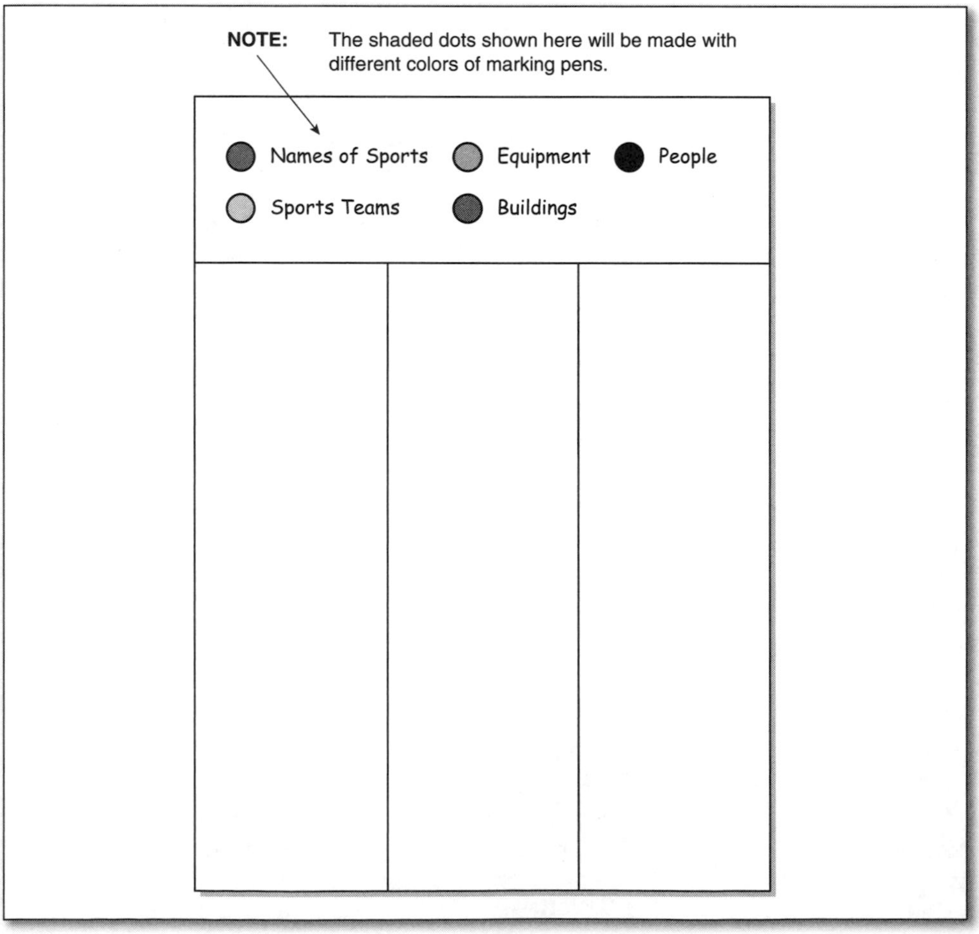

NOTE: The shaded dots shown here will be made with different colors of marking pens.

● Names of Sports ● Equipment ● People

● Sports Teams ● Buildings

Part 3: Classifying and Diagramming—*Emphasis on Complexity, Analysis, and Deductive Reasoning*

Step 1: Using a separate piece of paper, students choose one of the categories and look at all the words for that category (ones that have the same color dot).

Step 2: They select about six to eight words to use in creating a classification diagram. This classification diagram will follow a logical line of reasoning for sorting the words, until there is only one box at the bottom where each of the six to eight words is printed.

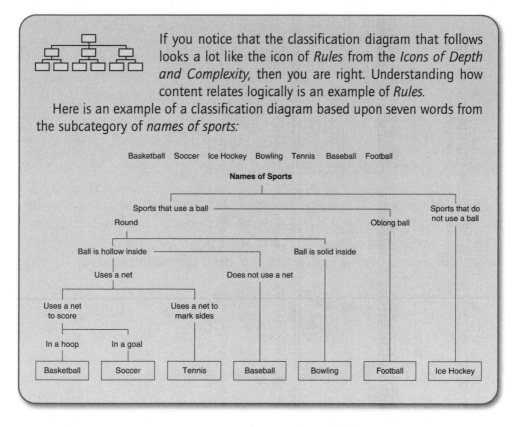

Students can sort according to the number of players on a team, what the playing field looks like (court, rink, or field), and so forth. The diagram will not look the same every time, depending upon how students sort or *classify* the information.

MODIFYING THE PROCESS

Sometimes teachers will give the students a set of eight words to sort instead of having them determine their own list from a broad topic. This modified lesson encourages analytical thinking but does not give students an opportunity to *drain their brain* of what they know about a topic. I suggest using both parts of the lesson for maximum learning. In the interest of time, teachers may have students sort only seven or eight words from the list they created. More words could be sorted, but it takes quite awhile. Years ago, I had students create a classification diagram using about 20 of the words. This was a multiday project and very rigorous.

FILLING IN A BLANK DIAGRAM

Another modification of *Concept Development* is to provide students with the classification diagram *without* the words at the bottom. It is their job to place a word in the bottom box that fits the criteria of the diagram. For example, tennis is a sport that uses a net to mark sides and for scoring. It also uses a hollow ball that is round. Is there another sport that fits those criteria? How about volleyball? Is there another sport that uses a hollow, round ball but does not use a net? How about kickball? Now you try it. Ice hockey doesn't use a ball in the game. Can you think of another sport that fits that criterion?

SOME FINAL THOUGHTS

Both *Word-Links* and *Concept Development* relate to the four areas of differentiation, to Bloom's Taxonomy, and also the *Icons of Depth and Complexity.* The first part of each lesson relates to the icon of *language of the discipline,* while the second part of both lessons relates to the icon of *rules.*

I share this information with you because it is important to see the interconnectedness of all of the instructional strategies presented in this book. Are you seeing the philosophy that forms the foundation of this book? Everything is related and connected. The brain is looking for patterns and relationships. It's the *big idea* of this book. I hope you are beginning to see it.

The next chapter explores *evaluative* questioning. These questions require students to make judgments about ethical issues and explain the rationale for their decisions.

7 Questioning Strategies in Evaluative Thinking Using Moral Dilemmas

INTRODUCTION

As you recall, *ethics* is one of the *Icons of Depth and Complexity*. Discussing *ethics* is an important part of understanding a topic, issue, person, or event in *depth*. Gifted youngsters have a strong desire to discuss ethical issues. James Webb, in his book *Guiding the Gifted Child* (1982), writes at length of the importance of supporting the social and emotional needs of the gifted. He shares that gifted students often display a heightened sense of moral justice and a desire for the world to be fair. Many of our gifted students become cynical and sarcastic as they grow older and realize that the world may not be a fair and just place. Bad things do happen to good people and vice versa. All students benefit when they are given opportunities to discuss issues of right and wrong because it helps them look at real-life problems from multiple perspectives, listen to others, and then formulate their own opinions.

FINDING MORAL DILEMMAS

There are many strategies teachers can use to address *moral development*. Obviously, teaching a particular moral position is not permissible within the public schools and teachers should remain objective. The best place to find moral dilemmas is in the content students are taught. Characters in most novels, stories, or selections from reading anthologies have moral issues to resolve and these are great for students to discuss or debate. History and science abound with moral issues as do current events. Social issues that occur daily on the playground are another source of real-life dilemmas to discuss.

With all the sources available to teachers from the content they are teaching, I still get requests to provide them with dilemmas that are appropriate for discussion with their students. The next section offers a selection of moral dilemmas, many of which I have used for discussion with teachers and administrators attending my seminars. Teachers may want to increase the *depth* of discussion by having students apply Kohlberg's *Stages of Moral Reasoning* (Kohlberg, 1976), described later in this chapter, as they ponder dilemmas from the next section.

A SELECTION OF MORAL DILEMMAS

1. The sheriff in a small town is guarding the courthouse against a mob about to storm it by force in order to capture a prisoner just arrested for a particularly heinous crime. The mob wants to lynch the prisoner without a proper trial. If the mob is frustrated, many people may be killed in the ensuing riot. There is a real possibility that, if the mob storms the courthouse, the sheriff and his deputy might be killed. Should the sheriff deliver the prisoner to the mob?

2. Should the wealthiest members of society pay for the poorer members of society through higher taxes?

3. A man has been sentenced to prison for robbery and admits guilt for the deed. "But," he argues, "I've never done anything like this before and never would do anything of the kind again. I'm not insane or a danger to society. My wife and children depend on me for support. You can keep the matter out of the newspapers and no one except you will ever know that you have released me." Assuming his statements are factual, should he be released?

4. A rich man and a poor man commit the same type of crime. The rich man is fined $10,000 while the poor man is sent to jail for one year. Is this fair?

5. You are on a country road and see two neighboring farmhouses on fire. One is yours and the other belongs to a new couple who have just moved in. Your wife and child are at home, as are your neighbors. You can only save one house. Which do you save?

6. You run an orphanage and have had a hard time making ends meet. A car dealership offers you a new van worth $20,000 for free if you will falsely report to the government that the dealership donated a van worth $40,000. You really need the van and it will give you an opportunity to help the children. Do you agree to take the van and make the false report?

7. You are shopping and see a woman stuffing a pair of stockings into her purse. Do you report her?

8. You are a passenger in a taxi. You notice that the driver is texting on his cell phone and driving unsafely. Do you report his actions to the company knowing that they will fire him?

9. You are waiting with a few other people to get on a bus. The bus pulls up and, while everyone is boarding, the driver goes into the convenience store to get coffee. You are the last to get on the bus. Do you pay your fare?

10. In Dostoyevsky's novel, *Crime and Punishment,* the main character plans and carries out the murder of an old woman who has a considerable amount of money in her apartment. After killing her, he steals the money. He argues that she is a malicious old woman, petty, cantankerous, and scheming, useless to herself and society, and her life causes no happiness to herself or others (all of which happens to be true). In addition, her money, if found after her death, would only fall into the hands of cheats and chisellers who have no more right to it than he does (which also happens to be true). He plans to use it for his education. Is his action justified?

11. On the street, you discover a wallet with identification and $500 in bills. Do you return the wallet and money to the owner?

12. It is 3 a.m. and you are late getting home. As you approach the intersection you notice that no one is around. Do you drive through the red light?

13. As a nurse, you are the last person to see Mr. Doe alive before he dies in the hospital. You believe that he has become mentally incompetent in the last few hours and in that time he has rewritten his will. In the new will he viciously attacks each member of his adopted family and reveals that he actually was born a woman. He then cuts every family member out of the will, leaving his fortune to a psychic chat line. Mr. Doe asks you to

make sure that the new will gets to his lawyer. You are sure that the document will most likely be thrown out of court, but in the interim, it will cause considerable damage to Mr. Doe's family. Do you carry out Mr. Doe's last request?

14. Would it be justifiable to whip pigs to death if more succulent pork results from this process, giving consumers of pork more pleasure?

15. Should the theft of $1,000 be punished more severely than the theft of $100?

16. Why should attempted murder be punished less severely than a successful murder?

17. Is it acceptable to use physical torture if it is the only means available to find out where in New York City terrorists have planted a bomb?

18. Joe is a 14-year-old boy who wants to go to soccer camp. His father promised him he could go if he saved up the money it would cost. Joe worked hard at extra jobs and saved up the $300 to go to camp, plus a little more. However, just before camp was going to start, his father changed his mind. His father wanted to go with his friends on a special fishing trip so he told Joe to give him the money. Joe is thinking of refusing to do so. What should Joe do?

19. Crystal is a fifth grader who was collecting tickets at a crowded school event. An adult couple slipped their way past Crystal and into the event without paying. Crystal was extremely upset that this occurred. She thought of confronting the adults. What should she do?

20. You are on a boat. Nearby are two large rocks filled with people waiting to be rescued. There are five people on one rock and four on the other. The tide is coming in and threatening to drown everyone. Your boat cannot rescue both groups. If you try, your boat will flood and you will drown with the rest. You can rescue one of the groups, but by the time that you return for the other group, they will have drowned. Which group do you rescue?

21. Sam is a 10-year-old fourth grader. He and Zeb are staying after school to finish some work. The teacher is in the hall talking to a parent. Zeb sees Sam take two items from a reward box. Sam is a bully and tells Zeb that he and his friends will beat Zeb up if he tells the teacher. The teacher returns to the room. What should Zeb do?

22. Theresa is a fifth grader. Her dad has been drinking beer at Uncle Ted's house. He staggers to the car and yells at Theresa to get in the car to go home. Theresa doesn't want to get in the car. What should Theresa do?

23. Kerri was absent from school one day because she went shopping in the city with her mom. She had a project that was due the day of her absence and she wants to turn it in later. Her mother is willing to write her an excuse and say that she was sick. Should she have her mother write the excuse and turn it in to the teacher?

24. John has been bothered by Tim who is a bully. John's father told him to hit Tim back if Tim starts a fight again. Tim pushes John down on the way to school. At recess Tim hits John again. John sees the yard duty teacher nearby and knows that if he hits Tim, he'll get caught and probably be suspended. If he doesn't stick up for himself, his dad will be disgusted with him. What should he do?

25. Jack and Billy are 10-year-old fifth graders. Jack claims that Billy is wearing Jack's sweatshirt that he has lost. The teacher discusses the situation with both boys and each is adamant that the sweatshirt belongs to him. The teacher asks each boy to have his mother write a note that the sweatshirt belongs to him. Both boys bring in notes saying that the sweatshirt is theirs. What should the teacher do now?

26. Sandra was struggling in eighth grade. She was undersized and poorly dressed but always came to class and worked hard. She made a "C" in math during the first nine weeks. At the second quarter, she had a "C" or above in every class but math, which she failed. When she saw the report card before going home, she threw herself in the corner next to a cabinet and sobbed. "He'll beat me! My dad will kill me!" Her teachers looked at Sandra and at each other in alarm. They quickly discussed ways to handle the situation. What should they do?

For more moral dilemmas, check out *The Daily Dilemma* at http://www.goodcharacter.com.

KOHLBERG'S STAGES OF MORAL REASONING

Lawrence Kohlberg, professor at the University of Chicago, is best known for his *Theory of Moral Development* (Kohlberg, 1976). From his research, he identified six stages of reasoning and believed that we all go through stages of moral reasoning sequentially, without skipping a stage, from infancy to adulthood. As a student of Piaget's developmental approach, he believed that people are not able to understand moral reasoning more than one stage ahead of their own.

Through his research, Kohlberg theorized that children learn moral behavior by watching how their parents handle moral issues and by discussing issues of right and wrong with parents, teachers, peers, and mentors. Kohlberg's theories have been criticized by some because of their *Eurocentric* view of right and wrong. In the lessons presented here, there is no attempt to label students at a certain stage on Kohlberg's scale. The goal of these lessons is not to teach moral or ethical behavior. The intent is to analyze the situation under discussion and describe various responses to each scenario, noting how they relate to the various stages Kohlberg identified. For example, what would a Stage 1 response be? Do you see how someone who is a Stage 4 might respond to the same dilemma? Kohlberg's *Stages of Moral Reasoning* are outlined here:

KOHLBERG'S STAGES OF MORAL REASONING

What Children Generally Do:

Stage 1: **Right** is what you do to avoid being punished.
Rules are obeyed to avoid getting in trouble or reprimanded.

Stage 2: **Right** is what gets you what you want.
Rules are obeyed to satisfy your own needs.

What Most of Us Generally Do:

Stage 3: **Right** is what pleases others. (peer pressure)
Rules are obeyed to gain approval from others.

Stage 4: **Right** is showing respect for authority and maintaining the social order.
Rules are obeyed to uphold the law.

What Some of Us Do:

Stage 5: **Right** is what is critically examined socially.
Rules are obeyed because they reflect upon certain agreed upon principles of society.

Stage 6: **Right** is what is ethical and respects human worth.
Rules are obeyed to avoid self-condemnation.

What follows are the explanations I use when discussing each of these stages with teachers and students to help them better understand Kohlberg's hierarchy.

THE MEANING OF KOHLBERG'S STAGES

Stage 1

This is what little kids do. They do the *right* thing to avoid getting punished. Have you ever watched *Supernanny* on television? She uses the *naughty chair* or the *reflection room* when children misbehave. Children or adults who operate their lives at this stage of moral reasoning do the *"right"* thing so that they don't get in trouble. Now, just when you think that kids are the only ones at this stage, think about the last time you were on the interstate and saw a highway patrolman approaching. You instinctively slowed down, right? Did you slow down because you were concerned about the safety of the passengers in your vehicle, or was it so you wouldn't get a ticket? If the answer is the latter, then that is Stage 1 behavior.

Stage 2

People who are at Stage 2 do the *right* thing to get something for themselves. "I'll be good in the store if you buy me something," says the child to his mom. "I'll be your friend if you give me what's in your lunch." "I'll invite you to my party if you bring me a present." Pretty immature, right? Well, how about this one. A colleague was asked to take a teacher's class for the last half hour of the day because the teacher had become ill and there wasn't enough time to get a substitute. When the sick teacher returned to work the next day, the colleague said, "I watched your class for a half hour so that you could go home early, so you *owe* me a half hour. You can watch my class for a half hour so I can go to the dentist." Whether you agree or not with the colleague's actions, they represent Stage 2 of moral reasoning. In *Charlotte's Web*, Templeton the rat is a classic Stage 2. He agrees to help Charlotte gather words for her web, but only if he gets first chance at the food in the trough. Stage 2 people believe, *I'll do the right thing, but I need to get rewarded for it.*

Stage 3

We've heard students say, "But everyone else is doing it! I'm not the only one." People who operate at Stage 3 generally do what the group does. The *rightness* or *wrongness* of their actions is dependent upon what everyone else is doing. This is the thinking that goes on with *looting*. To celebrate the Lakers winning the NBA championship, hundreds of people proceeded to break windows and steal from the stores surrounding Staples Center. Their reasoning: *everyone else is doing it.* What about people who lie on their income taxes because they believe everyone else does? What about those who simply go along with what their friends are doing without even thinking about the alternatives? Being accepted often is more important than doing what is *"right."* Peer pressure among adolescents is an example of Stage 3 behavior; so is gang mentality. Sometimes the issue isn't that critical, but what if it involves the treatment of certain groups of individuals? A principal once asked a teacher to change a high school student's grade so that the student would be eligible to play football, making the comment, "I can count on you to be a *team player,* can't I?" Sometimes the issue is very grave. Hitler appealed to Stage 3 mentality as he inflamed the Germans against the Jews prior to World War II.

Stage 4

Kohlberg believed that most of us operate at a Stage 4. People do the *right* thing because the law says it's the right thing to do. Those of us who are law-abiding citizens operate at a Stage 4. We want the social order to be maintained. However, from time to time the law may be wrong. The Civil Rights movement of the 1960s sought to change many of the laws that were common in the South. People who believe that their government is always right might fall into Stage 4. Those who evoke the law as their reasoning for doing the *right* thing are at Stage 4. Promises should be kept, not because it is the *right* thing to do but because a promise is a verbal agreement that is legally binding.

Stage 5

People who make moral decisions at Stage 5 do so based on agreed upon principles of society. Kohlberg notes that sometimes these principles have their roots in religious beliefs: *Honor Thy Father and Thy Mother, Thou Shall Not Kill, Thou Shall Not Steal,* and so forth. The *Golden Rule* might be cited as an agreed upon principle of society. People who operate at Stage 5 make decisions based upon principle and not upon what others say or the desire to get something for themselves. There are many controversial issues facing society today. People who decide what they believe about these issues and base their decisions upon a principle are at Stage 5, *regardless of the decision they choose.* People who are prochoice can be at Stage 5 and those who are antiabortion also can be at Stage 5. However, what if the prochoice person and the antiabortion person choose to act violently and assault someone who disagrees with them? Then neither person is acting at Stage 5 because an agreed upon principle of society is to do no harm to another person.

Stage 6

Have you ever asked yourself what the long-range implications would be regarding a decision you were about to make? Have you ever asked yourself if the decision you are making would make someone's life better or if it would make someone's life worse? Have you ever asked yourself if the decision you are making respects yourself or others? These are the questions people ask when they are operating at Stage 6 of moral reasoning. These questions explore implications, ramifications, and whether the resulting decision would be respectful of people. Telling someone a secret you have been sworn to keep to yourself might involve much soul-searching. If you decide to tell someone the secret, are you doing so just to spread gossip, or are you doing so because that person's life will be affected by implications of the secret? People who operate at Stage 6 put human worth before themselves. For example, Sydney Carton, in *A Tale of Two Cities*, sacrifices himself so that his look-alike, Charles Darnay, can continue his efforts to help the underground resistance during the French Revolution. Remember the quote, "It is a far, far better thing that I do, than I have ever done . . . ." What about someone who steals to help feed his starving children? It could be argued that such actions respect human worth, even though the civil and moral laws dictate, "Thou Shall Not Steal."

STEPS IN TEACHING A MORAL DILEMMA LESSON

Once teachers have a basic understanding of Kohlberg's stages, they can present a moral dilemma to the class. I use the following steps when presenting this lesson model:

1. The dilemma is presented to the class.

Teachers hand out a copy of the scenario or put it on the overhead projector. Here is a classic Kohlberg dilemma to discuss:

> Joe is a 14-year-old boy who wants to go to soccer camp. His father promised him he could go if he saved up the money it would cost. Joe worked hard at extra jobs and saved up the $300 to go to camp, plus a little more. However, just before camp was going to start, his father changed his mind. His father wanted to go with his friends on a special fishing trip so he told Joe to give him the money. Joe is thinking of refusing to do so. What should Joe do?

2. The class reads the dilemma aloud and the teacher asks students to present the facts in the scenario.

Facts are facts; they are not opinions. Teachers help students identify the facts, without drawing any conclusions. The facts are listed here:

> - Joe is 14.
> - Joe wants to go to camp.
> - His father promised him he could go if he earned the money.
> - Joe worked hard and earned the money.
> - His father changed his mind.
> - His father tells Joe to give him the money so he can go on a fishing trip with friends.
> - Joe is thinking of refusing to give his father the money.

3. The teacher tells students to pretend that they know Joe and that Joe has asked them for advice. The teacher tells students they each are to write a letter telling Joe what he should do under the circumstances presented.

Students are instructed not to confer or discuss with each other what they are suggesting to Joe. The teacher reminds the students that the letter *must* tell Joe *why* he should do what they have suggested to him. It isn't enough to simply tell Joe, "Give your father the money," or "Don't give your father the money." It is the *why* that is the important part of a moral dilemma.

4. Students share their letters with a partner or in small groups. The teacher reviews the six *Stages of Moral Reasoning* with the class and asks students to identify at which of the stages each of their responses would fit.

Here are some sample responses:

STAGE 1 RESPONSE:

> Joe should give his father the money because any dad that would make his son give him the money is not to be trusted. He might hurt Joe or do something awful to him. Give your dad the money to avoid his wrath! (You do the right thing to avoid punishment.)

STAGE 2 RESPONSES:

Joe should negotiate with his dad and tell him that he can have the money if he can go along on the fishing trip with his father. -**OR**- Joe definitely should tell his father that he won't give him the money because the money belongs to him; however, he could loan his dad the money with interest! (Right is what gets you what you want.)

STAGE 3 RESPONSES:

Joe should give his dad the money because that's what will make his father happy. Maybe his dad will be proud of him and appreciate him more. -**OR**- Joe shouldn't give his father the money because Joe's friends will think he's a *wuss* and make fun of him. (Right is what pleases others.)

STAGE 4 RESPONSES:

Joe should give his father the money because boys are supposed to do what their fathers tell them to do. -**OR**- Joe shouldn't give his father the money because a promise was made and a promise is legally binding. (Right is what keeps the social order.)

STAGE 5 RESPONSES:

Joe should give his dad the money because he should honor his father, an agreed upon principle of society. -**OR**- Joe shouldn't give his father the money because another agreed upon principle of society is that the money belongs to the person who earned it. (Right is based on agreed upon principles of society.)

STAGE 6 RESPONSES:

Joe should give the money to his father graciously and explain to him that although he doesn't agree that his father deserves the money, he will give it to him out of respect for the man who raised him. He will give it to him willingly and with no strings as a gift. It would be his great pleasure to do so. -**OR**- Joe should not give the money to his father because his father is not acting in a manner that deserves respect, and for Joe to have any self-respect, he cannot give in to an unreasonable demand.

5. The teacher selects several students to read their letters and conduct a class discussion about the dilemmas, including how the solutions each relate to the six *Stages of Moral Reasoning*.

It is important that teachers not label students as operating at a specific stage. Instead, teachers should focus discussion on the responses as they help students identify at which stage of moral reasoning each of the responses falls. A caution for teachers: it's not appropriate to tell the class what you would do with a particular dilemma. It is better to encourage students to discuss the dilemmas with their parents or to have a family discussion on the topic.

A DIAGRAM FOR ANALYZING DILEMMAS

The following is a diagram I created to use with students to help them analyze moral dilemmas. They choose an issue faced by a character in a story or novel and then determine which of the four areas, shown in the diagram, best describes the dilemma. Sometimes they can find issues related to one dilemma in all four areas:

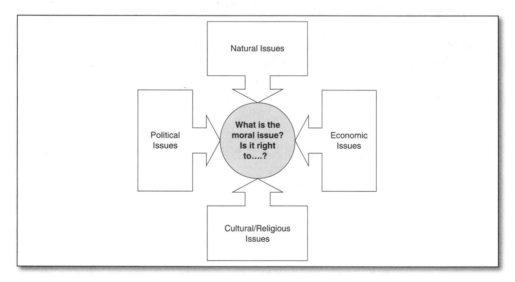

SOME FINAL THOUGHTS

While parents should be the primary influence for teaching their children right and wrong, students also observe how teachers act and behave on a daily basis, so we become important role models for ethical behavior. It's not just what we say but also what we do that has an impact on students. Asking students to discuss issues of right and wrong, while giving them a framework for this discussion in the safe atmosphere of the classroom, is essential to evaluative thinking. In the next chapter you are shown how to conduct Socratic discussions with your students. Many of the topics appropriate for a Socratic lesson contain moral dilemmas.

8 Questioning Strategies Using Socratic Reasoning

INTRODUCTION

Socratic questioning techniques are based upon the style of questioning presented in *The Dialogues of Plato* written over 2000 years ago. In this book, Plato recounts how his teacher, Socrates, led him to deeper understandings about philosophy, life, and science. For centuries, this style of questioning was part of a clas- sical education. During the 1960s and 1970s, through the Junior Great Books program, it was revived as an instructional strategy. Teachers and parents who were trained in this program used short literary selections to question students using the Socratic Method, a technique based upon the questioning style of Socrates. Although it was early in my career that I completed the Great Books training, my interest in the Socratic Method was rekindled several years ago when I was a presenter at a conference on critical thinking. While there, I happened to attend a seminar on Socratic questioning techniques, conducted by Dr. Richard Paul from Sonoma State University, and I was hooked! I believe that all teachers should have an understanding of Socratic questioning techniques and be able to use them to conduct a Socratic seminar. In this chapter, you will learn how to take a strategy originally designed for a small group of students and present it to the entire class.

SOCRATIC TEACHING

Socratic Dialogues are a style of questioning that continually asks students to *define* the meaning of the words they choose. If students say that a character in a story is *mean*, then a Socratic teacher would ask them to define what is meant by *mean* and give examples from the source on how that definition matches the actions of the character. To further expand thinking, the teacher might have students find examples from the story that demonstrate how the character also was kind, in order to help students see another perspective. When using Socratic techniques, it's important that the teacher does not represent any point of view. The teacher's goal is to have students *reflect* upon the statements they make and to substantiate the statements with information that is factual, not emotional. Socratic questioning causes students to think more carefully about their opinions and to base these opinions upon fact. Here we quote Socrates, using the Greek alphabet, of course:

Μυχη οφ ωηατ ωε τηινκ ωε κνοω ωε ονλψ
ηεαρ ανδ Βελιεϖε. Μυχη οφ κνοωλεδγε ισ
βασεδ υπον βελιεφ ρατηερ τηαν φαχτ.*

SOCRATIC TEACHING AND PHILOSOPHY

When teachers use Socratic techniques, they enter the world of philosophy, a subject not often taught in elementary or middle schools today. Historically, the *Sophists* were learned men in ancient Greece who were known for their love of learning, thus the term *philosophy* (*philo* meaning *love* and *sophy* representing *knowledge*). The four branches of philosophy are shown in the following diagram:

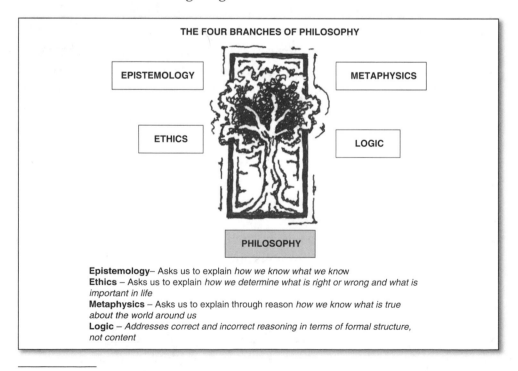

THE FOUR BRANCHES OF PHILOSOPHY

EPISTEMOLOGY

METAPHYSICS

ETHICS

LOGIC

PHILOSOPHY

Epistemology– Asks us to explain *how we know what we know*
Ethics – Asks us to explain *how we determine what is right or wrong and what is important in life*
Metaphysics – Asks us to explain through reason *how we know what is true about the world around us*
Logic – Addresses correct and incorrect reasoning in terms of formal structure, not content

---

*Much of what we think we know we only hear and believe. Much of knowledge is based upon belief rather than fact.

It is the intent of Socratic reasoning to help students examine questions in any of these four branches of philosophy. The goal is not to create a separate course in philosophy (although that would be pretty cool if you could do it!). Rather, the intent is to help students become more logical thinkers by using a specific set of techniques.

> To help remember the three great philosophers, picture a hot tub. Now imagine three very old men in the hot tub.
> The men are **S**ocrates, who taught **P**lato, who taught **A**ristotle. The first three letters of their names spell **SPA!**

THE ATTRIBUTES OF LOGICAL THINKERS:

- **Stick to the facts**—Logical thinkers look only at the evidence presented.
- **Argue the point, not the person**—Logical thinkers do not attack the person but stick to the points without getting personal.
- **Are skeptical, even of the teacher**—Logical thinkers question authority and aren't afraid to verify information, even from teachers and parents.
- **Are open to different points of view**—Logical thinkers are open to opinions of others and are willing to listen to opposing viewpoints.
- **Stay objective**—Logical thinkers keep biases out of the argument. They look at issues as objectively as possible.
- **Criticize pragmatically**—Logical thinkers learn how to criticize politely. They use humility and decorum when disagreeing with someone.
- **Are not hasty**—Logical thinkers are willing to ponder an issue, rather than rushing to judge.
- **Are not afraid of ideas**—Logical thinkers know that ideas cannot hurt us. They are not afraid to discuss ideas that may be difficult to understand.
- **Strive to understand, not always to be understood**—Logical thinkers are good listeners. Rather than trying to convince others of their points, they are willing and eager to listen to others and understand their points.

MODIFYING THE SOCRATIC METHOD TO FACILITATE CLASSROOM DISCUSSION

Since Socratic teaching was designed to be used with a small group of students, and teachers today seldom teach students in small groups, a new lesson structure is needed that keeps the essence of the concepts of Socratic teaching but is more practical within today's classroom structure. The following are the *Seven Steps of a Socratic Lesson,* as I have modified them from the original.

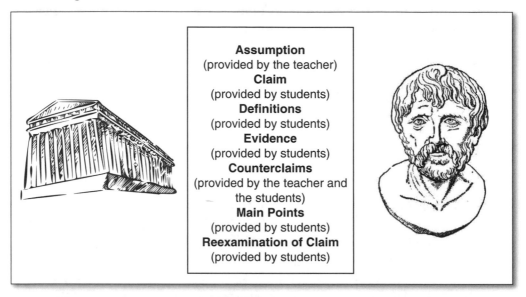

Assumption
(provided by the teacher)
Claim
(provided by students)
Definitions
(provided by students)
Evidence
(provided by students)
Counterclaims
(provided by the teacher and the students)
Main Points
(provided by students)
Reexamination of Claim
(provided by students)

THE SEVEN STEPS OF A SOCRATIC LESSON

1. The teacher makes an *assumption,* often stated in an "If . . . then" question: If this is true, then what might cause this to be true?

   o *If fairy tales are designed to teach young children lessons, then what is the lesson to be learned from Rumpelstiltskin?*
   o *If mathematics is part of the natural world and is all around us, then is it discovered or invented?*
   o *If authors write for a purpose, then what do you believe the author's purpose was in writing this story?*

2. The students discuss this assumption in table groups and make a *claim* as to what they believe to be the reason or answer to the assumption. A claim is a proposition that students believe to be true about something.

   We believe the lesson to be learned from Rumpelstiltskin is

   o *Don't be greedy.*
   o *Don't lie.*
   o *Don't make promises you can't keep.*

   During the *claim* stage, the teacher creates a chart so that each group can write their claim on the chart. (Each claim must be written in a complete sentence and students are to underline the key word or words in their claim.)

3. Students go back to their table groups and *define* what they mean by the key word(s) in their claim using working definitions, not dictionary definitions.

   o *We defined "greedy" as wanting more than you need.*
   o *We defined a "lie" as a deliberate falsehood and also not telling the truth (as a lie of omission).*
   o *We defined a "promise" as an agreement or contract about something you will do.*

   Students write their working definitions of key words on the chart.

4. Students select a spokesperson from their group to cite *evidence* to support their claim to the class. Students should be able to cite evidence by quoting the source material directly. During this time, the teacher asks questions to evoke discussion about any inconsistencies of their claim.

   o *You stated that everyone was greedy; however, if children are to learn not to be greedy, wouldn't you expect bad things to happen to all the greedy people? What happened to all the greedy people in the story?*

   o *If your claim is that people shouldn't lie, then why didn't anything bad happen to the miller or the miller's daughter because they lied? Why did Rumpelstiltskin die in the end, when he didn't lie, or did he?*

   o *If the miller's daughter promised to give Rumpelstiltskin her first born, did she break her promise? Did Rumpelstiltskin break his promise to her?*

5. Each group, in turn, has a spokesperson share the evidence. In response, the teacher might ask the class if anyone has a *counterclaim*, which is a response designed to find the flaws in the argument for each claim. If no one does, the teacher might ask more questions to help the class identify any flaws in thinking.

   o *Our group felt that our claim that the story is about greed is flawed, because all the greedy people get away with it except for Rumpelstiltskin. He was the only one who wanted to help the miller's daughter and he died a terrible death.*

   o *We think that Rumpelstiltskin is basically an evil person. The lesson must have something to do with him because he dies in the end and the others don't.*

6. A student spokesperson from each group then is asked to share the group's *main points,* a quick summary of why group members believes their claim is valid. No rebuttal is allowed at this time.

   o *We felt that the lesson here is not to lie. Everyone lied in the story and the biggest liar was Rumpelstiltskin because he wanted the baby from the beginning and only pretended to help the miller's daughter. Pretending to be nice to someone when you want something from them is the biggest lie you can tell. He is the most evil person in the story and should have died in the end.*

7. The final phase of a Socratic Dialogue is for students in each group to *reexamine the claim* in light of the discussion that has taken place to see if they wish to change it, modify it, or retain it. The final assignment is to write a paragraph or essay supporting their final claim, which includes citing evidence to support their final conclusion.

   o *Our group changed its mind. We thought the story was about greed, but now we think it's about keeping promises and being honest.*

SOME FINAL THOUGHTS

Socratic teaching does not always have to follow this formal approach. A teacher who has internalized this style of teaching uses the strategies on a daily basis. Whenever a teacher asks students to define what they mean, to provide evidence for their opinions, or to reexamine their original position in light of the statements and ideas presented by their peers, this is using the Socratic Method. A formal Socratic lesson, using the seven steps as presented earlier, is a great way for students to understand the discipline associated with philosophical thinking. However, don't feel that it is necessary always to approach every question in this formal manner.

If you are interested in more information about teaching philosophy or on using Socratic questioning, I recommend Dr. David A. White's book, *Philosophy for Kids* (2001).

9 The Creativity Connection

INTRODUCTION

As was discussed in Chapter 3, one of the four components of a *differentiated curriculum* is *novelty*. Novelty, as described earlier, is not the novelty or creativity of the teacher. Rather, novelty is the opportunity teachers provide for students to express their own creativity in novel or different ways. Let's take a moment and examine creativity as a brain function. If the brain is a pattern-seeking device that strives to find relationships between ideas and concepts, then it follows that creativity is the opportunity for the brain to find *unique* and *unusual* patterns and connections. *Creativity is the ability of the brain to see a variety of connections, pathways, and relationships.* Creativity is the outward manifestation of multiple pathways and connections. Creative people strive to find new ways of doing something, sharing something, teaching something, building something, or solving something. Creative people like to be different.

A FOCUS ON CREATIVE THINKING

Years ago, when I was teaching gifted students, a quote from Ralph Waldo Emerson had a real impact on me because it seemed to exemplify what I was striving to do as a teacher with my students:

> Do not go where the path may lead, go instead where there is no path and leave a trail.

When I was a teacher, each year I hung a banner in my classroom with Emerson's quote and discussed its meaning with my students. I explained that I would be encouraging them to use their creativity in some assignments so that they would have an opportunity to *do it differently* or to make it *unique* and *exceptional*.

CREATIVITY IN SCHOOLS TODAY

Creativity has, until recently, been valued in the American culture. We even gave it a term during the beginning of the last century: *Yankee ingenuity*. We held in high esteem the great thinkers and inventors of the early 20th century: Edison, Bell, Carnegie, Ford, the Wright Brothers, Walt Disney, Frank Lloyd Wright, and so forth. These were the heroes for several generations. We believed that the foundation of the American way of life rested with creative solutions to the problems that faced our nation. Schools provided students what was referred to then as a *balanced education*.

Times have changed and, as a result, so have our schools. With priorities on increasing academic performance, coupled with nationwide budget cuts to education, the new mantra has become, *if it isn't on the test, it isn't taught.*

Many elementary schools no longer find time to teach art, music, drama, dance, or even physical education on a regular basis. In some schools, science and social studies no longer are taught each day. In recent years, schools have narrowed their view of what once was considered a *balanced curriculum*, to focus almost exclusively on reading, writing, and arithmetic. Many students no longer have an opportunity to take part in drama productions, they aren't taught music appreciation, and art has morphed into coloring a worksheet. Students are taught various *formulas* for creative writing which has made writing anything but creative.

THINKING OUTSIDE THE BOX

Creative teachers are able to incorporate activities that encourage creativity into all areas of the academic program. We just need to think outside the box. We've all seen the logical thinking puzzle pictured here. The object is to connect the dots without lifting the pencil from the paper, using only four straight lines. Go ahead and see if you remember the *trick*. In order to accomplish the task, as you'll remember, it's necessary to extend the lines outside the box. This is what the business world means when it encourages *thinking outside the box.*

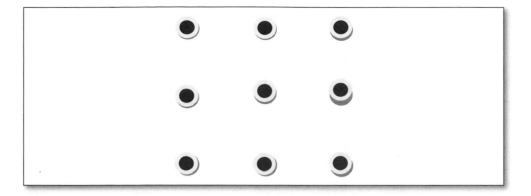

In his best-selling book, *A Whole New Mind: Why Right-Brainers Will Rule the Future* (2005), author Daniel Pink discusses the need for creative approaches to design a better economic plan for the 21st century. It's an entertaining book; you might want to pick it up. Businesses are begging for creative thinkers!

CREATIVE PEOPLE AT WORK

We often associate creativity with the arts or creative writing. Granted, students who can draw or write meaningful poetry may be labeled as creative; however, they may not be creative at all. When I was developing instructional materials for the Walt Disney Educational Media Company in the 1970s, I had the opportunity to work with some very creative people. However, not everyone who works for Disney is creative. At that time, most of the animation involved copying the work of others. It doesn't take creativity to draw Mickey Mouse; it's a discipline an artist learns from lots of practice. The real creative people were the writers and lead animators who devised the situations for the stories. My favorite times were discussions with the *Imagineers,* a very talented and creative group of men and women who designed the rides, attractions, motifs, and environments of the Disney theme parks. Many of them are artists, but just as many are engineers, architects, writers, accountants, and sociologists. What I noticed as I observed these creative people at work was that they started with *what they wanted to do* and then went backwards to *figure out how to do it.* They never let their lack of *know-how* act as a barrier to accomplish what they wanted to do. I remember a quote from Walt Disney that hung in the hallway of the Imagineering building, which said the following:

> **It's kind of fun to do the impossible.**

VALUING UNIQUENESS

One of the greatest gifts we can give our students is to revive the value we once placed on being different. We need to make it *okay* to do something in a unique way. We also need to teach students when to be precise and when to be creative.

OPPORTUNITIES FOR CREATIVITY IN THE CLASSROOM

In a classroom that values creativity, the teacher *underexplains* assignments, frequently encouraging students to complete projects in their own way. Open-ended projects can be leveled in such a way that more direction is provided for those who require additional guidance, while less explanation is given to students more capable of working independently. Here is an example of an open-ended assignment:

> Demonstrate your understanding of the Colonial Period in America in a creative and unique way. Show me what you know by creating something or by presenting information in an original way. Be accurate but do something different.

For some students, this is enough direction and will allow them to be creative. Other students might need some ideas for demonstrating their understanding in a creative way and the teacher might make some suggestions to get them started, such as a skit, a chart, a PowerPoint presentation, a display, a journal, and so forth. For students who need more guidance, the teacher could add some parameters, such as length or size, acceptable sources, or topics that should be addressed in the project.

Creativity also can be applied to something as logical and left-brained as mathematics by asking students to do things in a *different* way. Try asking, "Can anyone find another way to solve this problem?" Or spark creativity by saying, "What if you can't remember the formula for finding the area of a triangle? Demonstrate another way you might tackle this problem."

The daily interactions of students provide plenty of opportunities for teachers to encourage creative thought. "How will you do it next time?"

"What could you do to prevent this from happening again?" A teacher might guide students to settle their own disputes in creative ways. "The two of you need to sit here and discuss what happened, and then write down how you agree to resolve the situation."

CREATIVE BRAINSTORMING

In the business world, many companies hire consultants to work with their staffs to increase creativity. A popular activity often used at business retreats for this purpose is called *creative brainstorming*. While brainstorming activities are conducted in a variety of ways, I'll describe the one I've adapted over the years and use with groups. My suggestion is that you facilitate this activity with your students three or four times a year. It takes about 45 minutes to complete the entire process and it's an excellent way to encourage and value creative thinking.

CREATIVE BRAINSTORMING ACTIVITY

1. Students are shown a common, everyday object. They are to see how many uses they can think of for the object *other than its intended use.*

2. Students are placed in groups of three or four, with one of them selected as a recorder.

3. The student to the left of the recorder begins the activity. Students proceed in a clockwise direction as each student responds, in turn, to the prompt.

4. The recorder writes down all responses and also takes part in the activity. Students may not respond out of order, no duplicate responses are permitted, and no one is to comment on responses.

5. If a student cannot think of a response right away, the group waits until the student comes up with one. No one may skip a turn or take a turn out of order.

6. When the students understand the rules, the teacher shows them the object. It might be a comb, a paper clip, a toothbrush, a rubber band, a toilet paper roll, a baggie, anything that's handy.

7. The teacher reminds the students that they are to think of as many creative uses for the object *except its intended use.*

8. The teacher cautions the students to use quiet voices so other groups won't hear their ideas.

9. Students continue giving responses, moving around the circle, until the teacher stops the activity after *five minutes.* Prior to *calling time,* the teacher announces when there are two minutes left and then only a minute remaining.

10. When time is called, all responses stop and the recorders count up the number of responses.

THE THREE ASPECTS OF CREATIVITY

- Fluency – The number of responses made related to a prompt
- Flexibility – The number of original or unique responses related to the prompt
- Viability – The practicality of the response. Will it really work?

---

11. The teacher asks each group to share the number of ideas that were generated in the five-minute time limit. The group with the most responses earns the

FLUENCY AWARD

---

12. The teacher asks each table group to examine their list of ideas and to determine which two are the most *creative, unusual,* and least likely to be found on any other group's list. Each group then shares one of their two choices. If no other group has their idea on the first try, the second choice is not shared. If, however, another group has the same idea, then that group can share their second idea as a backup. If there are disputes as to whether the idea is the same or different, the teacher quickly decides. If no other group has the same idea, then that group receives the

FLEXIBILITY AWARD

13. The teacher tells the students that they have 20 minutes to pull together an *advertising campaign* to promote the use of the object in this new way. They need the following for their ad campaign:

- A product name
- A poster demonstrating how the product is used
- A jingle, song, or slogan that will help others remember the product
- One or more spokespersons to provide a commercial designed to sell the product to the class

14. The teacher reminds students to work quickly as they have only 20 minutes to complete the activity. The teacher announces that, after all presentations have been made, the class will vote on the product that it believes has the best potential for success as a marketable item. Individuals will vote but they may not vote for their group's product.

15. Students are given supplies needed for the activity, such as drawing paper, markers, and so forth, and the clock starts ticking. (Note: The teacher keeps out of this as much as possible, allowing the students to demonstrate their own novelty. This activity is meant to be done in class, not as homework. It's very important that students be expected to be creative on demand and not receive assistance from parents.)

16. At the end of 20 minutes, each group presents its product commercial. The class votes and the winning product receives the

VIABILITY AWARD

UNUSUAL PRODUCTS

An alternative to the *creative brainstorming* activity is more of an inductive approach. The teacher creates a list of unusual, nonsense products, or writes each one on a task card, or students can make up their own. The following example provides some suggestions:

SOME UNUSUAL PRODUCTS

- A soft kitchen table
- Spinach-flavored toothpaste
- A silent alarm clock
- A scratch and sniff automobile
- Soap that deposits dirt
- Disposable furniture
- Paper clothing
- Glue that doesn't stick permanently
- Deodorant that comes in colors
- Disappearing ink from ball point pens
- Talking refrigerators
- Frozen cereal
- Vegetable flavored ice cream

Each group selects one of the unusual products and creates an advertisement, to try and convince others that this is something they need to buy.

ENCOURAGING CREATIVITY THROUGH PROJECTS

Of course, the easiest way for students to demonstrate creativity is through their own projects related to content they are learning. We examine two kinds of projects here: projects that emphasize ideas and the creation of new ideas and projects that use materials and formats in new and creative ways.

IDEA PROJECTS

Idea projects focus on new ideas and conclusions drawn from information. These projects are more than a regurgitation of information gathered from the library or found on the Internet. Idea projects provide students a medium for drawing conclusions, comparing and contrasting, and taking information gathered and using it for another purpose. Here are some examples of idea projects:

- Compare George Washington and Dwight Eisenhower in at least five different ways.
- How is the Gold Rush in California like the Gold Rush in Australia? How were they different?

- Write a proposal of 10 ways to improve our school.
- What is the single most important invention ever created? Give reasons for selecting this invention.
- Our classroom's year-long theme is *systems*. Discuss how the system of government in the United States is like another system, such as the solar system, the human body, a computer, or the sewer system.

Did you notice that in each of the examples, the research the students conducted was used to present new ideas? Finding information is only part of what is expected. The assignment could have been to write a simple biography of George Washington. Instead, it was expanded so that the student had to find out about both George Washington and Dwight Eisenhower and then compare and contrast facts about them. This increases the opportunity for creative thinking while also adding depth and complexity.

PRESENTATION PROJECTS

The emphasis in *presentation projects* is on how the information is presented in a creative and unusual way. The intent of this type of project is to gather the information and to present it in an interesting and *unique* way. Here are some examples of presentation projects:

- Present a biography of George Washington using PowerPoint.
- Design an amusement park ride, suitable for a Disney theme park, based upon a novel you just read. Remember, the ride must contain elements to show that you have read the novel.
- Dress as a figure from history and share your experiences as if you were that individual.
- What chore do you hate doing more than any other? Now, design a tool or invention that will make that job easier for you. Build it or draw a diagram and tell how it works.
- Think like an entomologist and create an exhibit on beetles that the class can use in their learning.
- Create a museum display about ancient Egypt that covers four aspects of the Egyptian culture.
- Write a poem describing each of the planets to help us remember their characteristics.

- Build a model of Shakespeare's Globe Theatre and explain to the class how stage directions and scenery were used during this time period.
- Create an alphabet book on a particular subject, covering the topic from A to Z.

SYNECTICS LESSONS

Another form of creativity is *synectics*, a creativity technique similar to brainstorming but more formalized and rigorous, which was created by William Gordon (1961) and George Prince (1970). The word *synectics* is a joining of the words *synthesis* with *connections*. The Synectics Lesson Model encourages students to think, through metaphor or analogy, about the content. Asking students to respond to the riddle posed to Alice, in *Alice in Wonderland*, is an example of a *synectic connection*. The Mad Hatter asks Alice, "How is a raven like a writing desk?" While this is a rather ridiculous question, by asking it we engage our brains to see if there is a possible connection. Unfortunately, Alice couldn't think of any reason and asked the Hatter for the answer. He replied, of course, that he had absolutely no idea and if he did then why would he bother asking her in the first place. So much for riddles in Wonderland! After pondering the riddle, one of my students responded, "Edgar Allen Poe wrote *about* one *on* one." Pretty clever, don't you think? Here is a sample synectics lesson using the topic *gifted students:*

SYNECTICS LESSON: GIFTED STUDENTS

1. Decide what animal best represents a gifted student. (Example: *dolphin*)

2. List 10 words that describe how you might *feel* if you were a dolphin. Don't describe the animal; list what it would *feel like* to be that animal. (Example: playful, intelligent, talkative, trapped, endangered, friendly, helpful, social, free, defensive)

3. Examine your list and pick the two words you think are the most opposite. (Example: *playful* and *trapped*. It's hard to feel playful when you are trapped.) This is called a *compressed conflict.*

4. Set up an analogy connecting dolphins back to the topic *gifted students.* (Example: Like a dolphin, a gifted student feels both playful and trapped.)

5. Write a composition that elaborates on this connection. (example follows)

Gifted students are playful and creative and enjoy having fun just like a dolphin but they also are trapped in the prison of school. Dolphins are trapped when they are captured to perform at Sea World, just as gifted students are trapped when they are called upon to show how smart they are all the time. Dolphins in captivity never really can be themselves because of the nature of the aquarium where they are imprisoned. Similarly, the playful nature that is part of the joy of learning for the gifted may be taken away from them as they become trapped in boring classrooms and not given the freedom they need to explore the world on their own terms.

As students examine the relationship between the animal and the topic (in this example, *dolphins and gifted students*), other connections might be made. However, instead of comparing gifted students to an animal, the comparison could be to a plant, a kitchen appliance, a building, or anything else. If gifted children are compared to a building, the response might be this: "Gifted students are like a subway terminal because . . . ." The rest of the lesson proceeds in the same manner.

Synectics also can be used creatively in projects. Margee Fuller, a fourth-grade teacher, gave the following assignment to her students: *How is the California Mission system like the garden system we have at our school?* Since their year-long theme was *systems,* her students had acquired a lot of knowledge in this area and they also were familiar with the gardens at our school. By putting the two together, they shared six ways that the mission system was like the garden system. This is another form for using synectics.

Sometimes synectics lessons ask students to see what connections they can make from seemingly dissimilar words. A suitable description of synectics is *making the strange familiar and the familiar strange.* The following is another activity using synectics:

SYNECTICS ACTIVITY

The teacher writes an arbitrary array of dissimilar words on the board, such as the following example:

Elbow	Pencil	Snake	Clock	Underwear
Acorn	Snow	Lint	Video game	Fork
Envelope	Pumpkin	Collar	Spaghetti	Toothpaste

Students are invited to make a connection between any two words. Once the connection is made, the words are erased. The goal is to continue to make connections until there are three words left. Here are some examples:

- Elbow and spaghetti are connected because spaghetti is a kind of pasta and so is elbow macaroni.
- Underwear and lint can be connected because often they both are forgotten and left behind in the clothes dryer.

Now you try it. The final connection must be made with three words left at the end.

SOME FINAL THOUGHTS

Whenever we ask our students to *make it strange* or to come up with a unique way of doing something, we are valuing creative thought. Many students are reluctant to do things differently, fearing that the teacher or peers won't approve. Students need to know when it's appropriate to be creative and when it's not. I encourage you to make it appropriate to be creative from time to time in your classroom assignments.

10 Teaching Research Skills and Methods

INTRODUCTION

Research skills and methods are another important set of thinking skills we can teach our students. Throughout their educational careers, students are assigned reports. However, one can wonder how many teachers actually *teach* students the important elements of writing reports: how to take notes, finding information in the library or on the Internet, ways to organize information, preparing an outline, citing sources, and so forth. The skills associated with conducting research and writing a report must be taught. It's not enough to assign reports and projects.

FOCUS ON LEARNING

At the elementary level, often the physical appearance of the project takes precedence over the knowledge gained from the project. I'm sure the following true story will sound familiar to many teachers. When I was judging science fair projects at a local school, I was particularly interested in a well-constructed fifth-grade project on the uses of daphnia, a microorganism, in the purification of lake water. The project was beautifully presented, with colorful photos, organized charts, and carefully prepared documentation. However, when I asked the student to explain the project to me, the explanation was about how the project was assembled, with the help of a parent. The student couldn't explain any of the conclusions or what was learned from the project, but he suggested I talk to the father because he knew. Unfortunately, the appearance of this project had taken precedence over any knowledge to be gained from the project.

Now this kind of situation might not happen at your school. However, we teachers need to remember that the goal of research is to increase knowledge of the subject matter. Another goal is to teach our students how to *search* for information and ways to organize the information once it is gathered. Whenever parents are overly involved in school projects, they are depriving their children of learning the skills necessary to execute projects in the future. A teacher at one of my schools solved the problem by having the students do all their projects in class. At the beginning of the year, the quality of science projects wasn't as great as when students did the work at home with the help of parents, but it improved over the course of the year. However, the depth of learning students derived from creating their own projects at school was far superior. Students left that class at the end of the year really understanding how to set up a science investigation, including collecting and analyzing data, drawing a conclusion, and communicating their results.

RESEARCH SKILLS AND METHODS

The following outline of *research skills and methods* might help teachers determine the ones you want to stress in your classroom. Understandably, it is hard to cover them all, and some will probably have been mastered by students in previous years. Take a moment and put a check by the *five* that you believe are the most important at your grade level. Five seems to be a manageable number when trying to focus on a set of critical skills in this area. Remember, you will be *teaching* each one of the skills you choose. *Note taking* and *summarizing* seem to be two that most teachers include. However, your grade level and own expectations will determine your top five.

RESEARCH SKILLS AND METHODS

Accessing Information Skills

□ Knowing the parts of a book: table of contents, glossary, index, chapters, etc.
□ Finding a book in the library: card catalog, Dewey Decimal System, computerized accessing system
□ Using the Internet: search engines, refining searches, querying correctly
□ Differentiating fact from opinion
□ Determining authenticity

Organizing Information Skills

□ Summarizing
□ Paraphrasing
□ Taking Notes
□ Outlining
□ Creating a web or graphic organizer
□ Citing references: bibliography, footnotes
□ Organizing data around a topic

Presentation Information Skills

□ Pronouncing technical vocabulary correctly
□ Maintaining eye contact
□ Speaking from notes
□ Speaking with authority and with interest
□ Using a loud enough voice to be heard

EXAMINING A TYPICAL SCHOOL PROJECT

We are going to look at several projects, starting with an example of a typical elementary school project, a state report:

My State Report on _____:

1. Write a paragraph about the major geographic features of the state.

2. Find out what crops and products come from the state and write a paragraph about them.

3. Draw a map of the state labeling the following:

   a. The major cities, including the capital
   b. The major geographic features

4. Draw a picture of the state flower.

5. Draw a picture of the state bird.

6. Draw a picture of the state mammal.

7. Draw a picture of the state insect.

8. Pick a famous person from the state and tell why that person is important.

9. Find out when the state entered the Union.

10. Draw a picture of the state flag.

11. Draw a picture of the state seal.

12. Draw a picture of a favorite place to visit in the state.

13. Put your information in a notebook and make an attractive cover.

I don't want you to think that this project is bad, well, not *all* bad. I'm suggesting that it is not in keeping with what we would expect from a fourth- or fifth-grade student. Except for the fact that there is a lot of drawing taking place and not much writing, this project might work for a student who is at the novice stage of research skills. To meet the needs of our students of average and high ability, however, we need to take a more detailed look at *idea projects* and *presentation projects* and ways to use them to encourage critical thinking.

TWO KINDS OF PROJECTS TO MAKE KIDS SMARTER

Let's explore in more depth *idea projects* and *presentation projects*, along with some examples of each.

IDEA PROJECTS

The emphasis is on new thinking. Here are some examples:

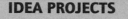

- A project that asks students to compare and contrast events, people, places, animals, ideas or concepts (e.g., comparing one U.S. state to another, using a Venn diagram, or to a foreign country, using a three-circle Venn)
  - A project that draws conclusions after presenting data or examples (e.g., a science project, a response to literature)
  - A project that presents original thinking in writing (e.g., poetry, suggestions, or proposals)
  - A project that encourages students to think like disciplinarians in the field and create something that is similar to what someone who studies the topic in the real world would do (e.g., the Revolutionary War from the perspective of an economist or the study of a character in a novel from the perspective of a psychologist or psychiatrist).

PRESENTATION PROJECTS

The emphasis is on presenting ideas in new and unusual ways using materials and forms. Here are some examples:

- Present the project in a pop-up book.
- Present the project in PowerPoint.
- Dress as a character or famous person to present the project.
- Create a game based upon the project.
- Write a play or a skit to present the project.
- Design an amusement park ride based upon the ideas in the project.
- Write a poem.
- Create a news report.
- Make a video.
- Write a song and sing it.

PRESENTATION VERSUS CONTENT

Many of the project ideas suggested here have been used by teachers for years. However, the challenge is to select projects that require both depth and complexity. Projects, if they are to have any meaning for our high-ability students, should mimic the work of scholars in the field. That doesn't mean projects have to be dull and boring, but we have to be careful not to let the outward appearance of a project surpass the research skills and methods used. If a student can complete a project without doing any substantive information gathering and organizing, then the project is not a worthy one. It often is the fault of the project and not the student. A diorama depicting a scene from a novel may not be the best project for a student because it could be completed without reading the book. A more appropriate project involving literature might be a literary analysis where the student does some comparing or contrasting of characters, theme, conflict, and so forth. Some of our students really enjoy making dioramas and might want to use them as projects in science or social studies.

Highly visual projects often have a greater appeal to teachers, and to students, than those requiring a lot of writing. Take a moment to reflect upon your own preferences. Do you give higher grades to the project that is visually pleasing? You might want to consider giving separate grades for presentation and content so that the project that is thoroughly planned and written receives appropriate acknowledgment.

ASSIGNING MEANINGFUL PROJECTS

One way to help teachers assign meaningful projects is to go back to the list of research skills and methods in this chapter. Could you assign an effective project that requires students to use the five key skills you chose from your list? Could you assign a project that incorporates these five skills as part of the rubric for grading the project so that students would be required to address them? This type of planning is called *backward mapping*. This process begins by identifying the skills you want the students to demonstrate and then looks backward to create a project assignment that requires students to use the identified skills. Most teachers start with an idea for a project rather than with the skills necessary for appropriate execution of the project. Instead of demonstrating the skills and methods of research as the goal of the project, the project itself becomes the goal.

Let's consider an example to clarify this procedure. If a teacher determines that note taking is an essential skill that students need for research, then the teacher needs to create a project assignment that requires students to turn in their notes prior to completion of the project. The teacher will want to see how the students took notes from reference books, lectures, media, and so forth, to see if they have learned this part of the process. Consequently, the students' notes should be allocated an adequate number of points toward the project grade because that is a skill the teacher wants to emphasize. The completed project then is based upon the organization of the students' notes.

USING RUBRICS TO EVALUATE PROJECTS

Rubrics are a critical component for evaluating projects. The rubric explains how the teacher will evaluate and grade the project. Teachers can design the rubric, the students can create the rubric, or one can be used or adapted from one of the many books devoted to rubrics. My recommendation is to create the rubric prior to having students begin the project so that the rubric can provide guidance for the project assignment.

My colleague, Marilyn Brown, created a great rubric for oral presentations which I've used and modified over the years and shared with other teachers. There are several reasons I like this rubric: It is divided into sections that represent the important parts of a project, it's easy to calculate a grade because the points total 20, it emphasizes the knowledge gained from the assignment, and it focuses on presenting the information in an interesting way.

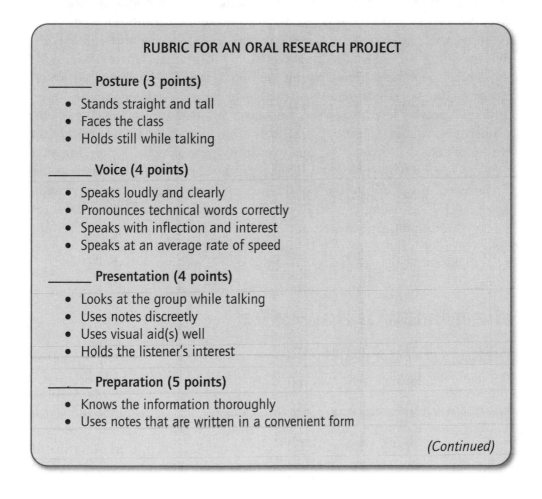

RUBRIC FOR AN ORAL RESEARCH PROJECT

_____ **Posture (3 points)**
- Stands straight and tall
- Faces the class
- Holds still while talking

_____ **Voice (4 points)**
- Speaks loudly and clearly
- Pronounces technical words correctly
- Speaks with inflection and interest
- Speaks at an average rate of speed

_____ **Presentation (4 points)**
- Looks at the group while talking
- Uses notes discreetly
- Uses visual aid(s) well
- Holds the listener's interest

_____ **Preparation (5 points)**
- Knows the information thoroughly
- Uses notes that are written in a convenient form

(Continued)

(Continued)

- Seldom looks at notes
- Appears to have practiced the report
- Acts interested in the information

_____ **Information (4 points)**

- Report is well organized and easy to follow
- Report contains most important facts
- Facts are accurate
- Unimportant details have been omitted

PEER, SELF, AND TEACHER EVALUATION

I recommend various kinds of evaluations for projects: self-evaluation, peer evaluation, and teacher evaluation. One evaluation strategy that has worked well is to give the rubric to four students at random. They each evaluate the oral report of a student and then discuss and collectively determine the score. This score is worth 50% of the student's grade, with the teacher's evaluation making up the other 50%. The student's self-evaluation, while not counting toward the grade, is used as a benchmark to see how it correlates to the peer and teacher evaluations. Some teachers have concerns about the validity of peer evaluation. However, I have found that students take this process seriously and are very objective, knowing that they also will be subject to random peer review. Some teachers have added a comment section on the back of the rubric where students are to provide one positive comment (no criticisms from students) about the presentation, project, or report. One teacher gives an extra two points to the student who volunteers to be the first to present the report so that the entire class can evaluate it as a way of learning how to score using the rubric.

THE PROBLEM OF PLAGIARISM

Plagiarism is a major problem in schools today. This is due, in part, to the Internet and the easy access to reports and papers. Students can go online and search for any kind of report, let's say a fifth-grade report on George Washington, five pages long. They will find several to download and claim as their own. Secondary teachers often utilize websites that can scan students' papers to check for excerpts that have been lifted from other documents without annotation. This practice has frustrated me as a teacher and administrator. I hate being the *plagiarism police.* I do have a solution which utilizes the *Icons of Depth and Complexity* and is plagiarism-proof, at least for the time being. Examples are shown here:

USING THE ICONS FOR REPORT TOPICS

Instead of a standard report on George Washington, students can investigate one or more of the following questions:

- Discuss the *changes over time* that George Washington experienced in his career related to at least three *ethical* issues that confronted him.
- Find four *details* in the life of George Washington that are part of our folklore and not actual fact. Relate these *details* to a *big idea* about heroes, both historic and modern.
- Compare George Washington to another military leader who was asked to become a political leader, such as Andrew Jackson, Ulysses S. Grant, or Dwight Eisenhower. How were the *patterns* of their lives similar?

By using the *Icons of Depth and Complexity,* we not only create plagiarism-proof papers, but we also generate topics that are far more worthy for our high-ability students than the traditional biography report that has been copied from encyclopedias for decades.

SELF-DIRECTED INDEPENDENT STUDY SKILLS

In addition to the goal of teaching students how to conduct and present research, another major goal for our gifted students is the development of self-directed, independent study skills. Barbara Clark and Sandra Kaplan included these skills as one of their 13 *principles of differentiation* for the gifted back in the early 1980s. Like academic skills, these also must be taught to students.

I remember directing our young son to clean his room. He disappeared into the black hole of toys, clothing, unmade bed, and several items I could not hope to classify. He emerged in about five minutes, with a big smile, to say he was finished. When my wife and I entered  the room, we didn't notice any change at all. The next time we knew better and my wife and son cleaned the room together. In this way, he learned what we expected a clean room to look like and how to go about organizing things, putting clothes in drawers, toys in the bin, and discarding trash. The same is true with the self-directed study skills. It's not enough to expect them; teachers must teach them. The following list is a suggestion of what these skills might include:

SELF-DIRECTED INDEPENDENT STUDY SKILLS

- Read a reference twice before asking what it means.
- Define a daily routine for completing homework.
- Use time wisely.
- Maintain focus.
- Get help when you need it.
- Break down projects into manageable steps.
- Know when to be precise and when to be creative.
- Match appropriate references to the appropriate question.
- Stay organized.
- Keep moving forward.

STRATEGIES FOR TEACHING STUDY SKILLS

As with the list of *research skills and methods,* teachers need to choose three to five of the skills from the list of *self-directed independent study skills.* Remember, if *organization (stay organized)* is a priority for the assignment, then teachers will need to show students what to do to *be organized.* A teacher who expects students to *be organized* has a format for notebooks, note cards, outlines, homework, and so forth. *Organization is reinforced* when the teacher has a schedule for students to submit their reports for review during various stages of development.

Teaching the skill of organization went a step further with Gil Brown, a teacher at Mariposa Elementary School. He had his students keep all their daily class assignments and homework in a specific sequence, using a three-ring binder with tabs. Each week, at random, he collected six to eight binders, which he reviewed for organization and completeness.

When I was a classroom teacher, one of my essential skills was to *maintain focus.* I intentionally taught students the behaviors exhibited by focused individuals: alert posture, eye contact, nodding of the head, and a well-placed, *"Um, very interesting"* when I said something particularly insightful! Students practiced being focused by *pretending* they were interested and behaving as though they were. Remarkably, students became more focused. Such is the power of suggestion on the brain!

A teacher in one of my seminars shared a strategy she uses. She selects a few of the *self-directed independent study skills* from the list and asks students to describe what the skills *look* like and *sound* like. An example she shared is the sound of a pencil scratching on paper, which can be an indicator that students are *using time wisely*. Hopefully, the scratches were related to the assignment!

The importance of teaching these skills cannot be emphasized enough. Some of our brightest students often are disorganized. In elementary school, a lack of organization may not manifest itself in poor grades; however, as tasks increase in complexity during high school and college, students who are not organized have more difficulty and become frustrated with school. A lack of organization is a contributing factor for students who drop out of school because they fall behind with assignments. Teaching students essential study skills helps them maintain their independence and focus through the normal distractions of college life.

TEACHING STUDENTS TO TAKE NOTES

Another essential skill we can teach our students is how to take appropriate notes. Teachers should address proper note-taking from lectures, textbooks, reference books, media, and even explanations the teacher scrawls on the board. Beginning in second grade, I believe that teachers should show students how to take notes off the board. One of my second-grade teachers was fond of saying to her students, "When my pen is moving on the whiteboard, yours should be moving on your papers. Sitting with your hands clasped in front of you will not get any work done. Keep the pencils moving!" She taught her class to copy into a composition book everything she wrote on the board. Some wrote more slowly and were told, "Write faster, don't worry about neatness, don't give up, you'll get it!" Her philosophy was *no excuses.* When students have difficulty doing something, they often rely on excuses as reasons for underperformance: "Don't expect very much from me, I'm hyperactive!" It's better to expect more from students, teaching them the skills needed to meet those expectations. Teachers who have whiteboards or *SMART Boards* are encouraged to use color, which is an excellent visual tool to help students track information. Alternating colors and highlighting key words in color are two techniques to use.

TAKING NOTES FROM A LECTURE

For centuries, lecture has been a fundamental way to impart information to audiences of students, especially in secondary schools, colleges, and universities. My suggestion is that teachers begin with short lectures to students in the elementary grades, at least once a week, to provide information on a curricular topic. Students need to learn how to take notes from a lecture, and the sooner they learn this skill, the better for them. However, taking notes from a lecture is quite different from taking notes from a text or reference book. The brain thinks like a *dendrite* looks, like the branches of a tree, or a web. As teachers are lecturing, initially they can display key information using graphic organizers for students to copy, providing less guidance as students become more adept at taking notes. Eventually, students will be able to design their own graphic organizers to help them organize and remember information as they listen to lectures and take notes on their own.

How long should lectures be? Remembering what we know about the brain, as described in Chapter 2, lectures should be no longer than the attention span of students, which is about three minutes more than their age. For fifth-graders who are about 10 years old, this means no more than 13 minutes of continuous listening; for middle and high school students, 15 to 20 minutes is the maximum. After listening for that amount of time, students need to engage in some output activity, such as responding to a question, summarizing with a partner, or repeating key words, before the lecture continues.

One of my favorite lectures is one I present about *Schloss Neuschwanstein*, the beautiful iconic castle in the Bavarian Alps, built by  "Mad" King Ludwig, which provided the inspiration for the castle at Disneyland. For my lecture, I display a blank graphic organizer on the overhead projector. I purposely do not give students the organizer on a worksheet because I want them to learn to take notes. As I present the lecture, I add information to the diagram, adding lines to show relationships so that students can see how their notes should look. At the end of the lecture, I give a short quiz, allowing students to use their notes. Because the quiz is designed to address the exact information I presented, my expectation is that every student achieves 100%.

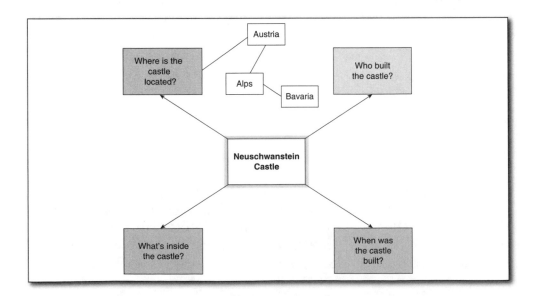

Once students become familiar with using graphic organizers, they can apply them when taking notes from a live speech or a recorded video or any other form of auditory presentation. I conclude each session with a short five-point quiz, always allowing students to use their notes. This technique is helpful to keep students focused, especially when they are watching a video. This strategy helps prevent students from being in the *Blockbuster mode*. This is the mode students tend to *settle into* when they watch a movie, video, or DVD in school. Someone always asks if there is popcorn or if they can sit on the floor. Watching a DVD in school is very different from renting one on Netflix.

TAKING NOTES FROM A TEXTBOOK

Note-taking from a textbook often is formatted in the standard outline form because textbook headings lend themselves to this type of organizer:

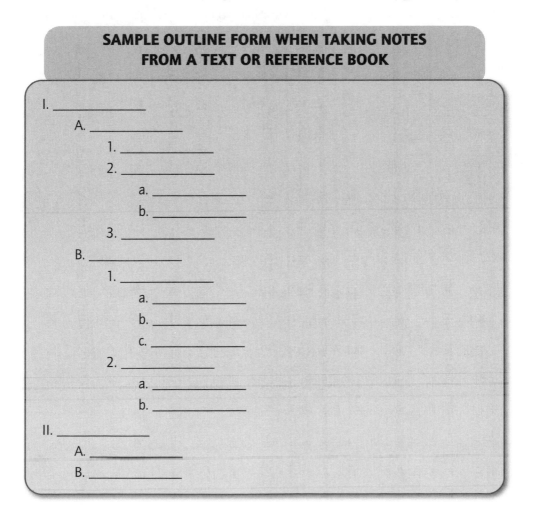

SAMPLE OUTLINE FORM WHEN TAKING NOTES FROM A TEXT OR REFERENCE BOOK

I. _____
    A. _____
        1. _____
        2. _____
           a. _____
           b. _____
        3. _____
    B. _____
        1. _____
           a. _____
           b. _____
           c. _____
        2. _____
           a. _____
           b. _____
II. _____
    A. _____
    B. _____

SOME FINAL THOUGHTS

Research projects provide an important method for students to synthesize information. Remember to make the focus of the project the content and presentation, rather than the appearance or display of it. Using the specific procedures and skills of research to enhance the knowledge gained from the project should be the main emphasis. In order for students to acquire necessary research skills, teachers must provide lessons on accessing, organizing, and presenting information.

Conclusion

We've reached the end of the book. However, it's actually only the beginning. Before you close the back cover, there are a few *big ideas* that I want you to remember:

- Providing rich, meaning-centered thinking activities should not be reserved for just our brightest students. All students benefit from thinking deep and complex thoughts.
- Remembering how the brain processes information will encourage you to expect your students to do most of the work: *Whoever does the work gets smarter!*
- The many strategies presented in this book can be used in isolation or in tandem. Give yourself permission to start slowly, but please start! There is no perfect time to present the *Icons of Depth and Complexity*, or *Themes*, or *Word-Links*, or *Language of the Discipline Cards*, or a *Taba* lesson . . . .
- The discipline of thinking cannot be overlooked. Require your students to justify their thinking with evidence. Call them on it when they don't.
- Creativity is just waiting to be released for so many of our students. Give them opportunities to show you what they have inside of them.
- Teach your students to be self-directed and independent learners. Require that they master the research skills through projects that are interesting, challenging, and fun.
- Finally, please enjoy our profession. Teaching is a most rewarding endeavor and it should be fun, not just for the kids, but for you too!

References

Adler, M. (1952a). *Great books of the western world* (54 vols.). Chicago: Encyclopedia Britannica.

Adler, M. (1952b). *The syntopicon: An index to the great ideas* (2 vols.). Chicago: Encyclopedia Britannica.

Caine, R., & Caine, G. (1990). *Making connections, teaching and the human brain,* Alexandria, VA: Association for Supervision and Curriculum Development.

Ceci, S. (2001). IQ Intelligence: The surprising truth. *Psychology Today,* July/August, 46–53.

Ceci, S. J. (1996). *On intelligence: A bio-ecological treatise on intellectual development* (2nd ed.). Cambridge, MA: Harvard University Press.

Clark, B. (1996). *Meeting the challenge: A guidebook for teaching gifted students.* Orangevale, CA: California Association for the Gifted.

Clark, B. (1997). *Growing up gifted* (5th ed.). New York: Prentice Hall.

Gordon, W. J. (1961). *Synectics: The development of creative capacity.* New York: Harper & Row.

Grun, B. (2005). *The timetables of history: A horizontal linkage of people and events.* New York: Simon & Schuster.

Harmin, M. (2006). *Inspiring active learning: A complete handbook for today's teachers.* Alexandria, VA: Association for Supervision and Curriculum Development.

Hart, L. (1983). *Human brain, human learning.* White Plains, NY: Longman.

Jensen, E. (1998). *Teaching with the brain in mind.* Alexandria, VA: Association for Supervision and Curriculum Development.

Jensen, E. (2008). *Super teaching* (4th ed.). Thousand Oaks, CA: Sage.

Kaplan, S., & Gould, B. (1999). *Frames: differentiating the core curriculum.* Chatsworth, CA: J Taylor Education.

Keirouz, K. (1993). Gifted curriculum: The state of the art. *Gifted Child Today,* 16(1), 36–39.

Kohlberg, L. (1976). Moral stages and moralization: The cognitive-developmental approach. In T. Lickona (Ed.), *Moral development and behavior: Theory, research and social issues.* New York: Holt, Rinehart & Winston.

Maker, C. J. (2005). *Teaching models in gifted education* (3rd ed.). Pro-ed Incorporated

Montgomery, M. (2006). *Math icon cards.* Chatsworth, CA: J Taylor Education.

Pink, D. H. (2005). *A whole new mind: Why right brainers will rule the future.* New York: The Penguin Group.

Prince, G. M. (1970). *The practice of creativity.* New York: Macmillan.

Slocumb, P. D., & Payne, R. K. (2000). *Removing the mask: Giftedness in poverty:* Highlands, TX: aha! Process, Inc.

Taba, H., Durkin, M. C., Fraenkel, J. R., & McNaughton, A. H. (1971). *A teacher's handbook to elementary social studies: An inductive approach* (2nd ed.). Reading, MA: Addison-Wesley.

Webb, J. T. (1982). *Guiding the gifted child: A practical source for parents and teachers.* Scottsdale, AZ: Great Potential Press.

White, D. A. (2001). *Philosophy for kids.* Waco, TX: Prufrock Press.

Wiggins, G. (1998). *Standards, not standardization.* Hoboken, NJ: John Wiley & Sons.

Wilkes, P., & Szymanski, M. (2009). *The deep and complex look book.* Chatsworth, CA: J Taylor Education.

Wolfe, P. (2001). *Brain matters: Translating research into classroom practice.* Alexandria, VA: Association for Supervision and Curriculum Development.

Index

CORWIN

A SAGE Company

The Corwin logo—a raven striding across an open book—represents the union of courage and learning. Corwin is committed to improving education for all learners by publishing books and other professional development resources for those serving the field of PreK–12 education. By providing practical, hands-on materials, Corwin continues to carry out the promise of its motto: **"Helping Educators Do Their Work Better."**